To my mother, Elizabeth "Betty" Newton, who loved only one person more than my dad and that, is Jesus.

"You have always been an inspiration and encouragement to me. My love for God's word was instilled in me at such an early age because I saw it have such an impact on your life. Thanks Mom for your example."

A note from Pastor Newton

It is my sincere desire that through the daily use of this resource you find peace in the storms of life, encouragement to walk in the Spirit, and a deeper relationship with our awesome God.

May God richly bless you as you enjoy moments with the Master.

Jim Newton

"I rejoice at thy word, as one that findeth great spoil."
Psalm 119:162

January 1
Genesis 1-3

Genesis 3:23-24
"(23) Therefore the LORD God sent him forth from the garden of Eden, to till the ground from whence he was taken. (24) So he drove out the man; and he placed at the east of the garden of Eden Cherubims, and a flaming sword which turned every way, to keep the way of the tree of life."

What a sad day for man, when God separates him from His presence. Sin separates us from God. Throughout the Old Testament this separation is seen in the Temple where the Holy of Holies is separated from the rest by the thick veil. No one is allowed in the Holy of Holies except the High Priest on the Day of Atonement and even then he must go through a major ritual to come into the presence of God. Oh, but thank the Lord Jesus, for in His death on the cross, the veil was torn open and through His sacrifice for sin we have been given access to the Father. What sin had destroyed, Jesus has restored!

Add your thoughts and/or prayer for the day

January 2
Genesis 4-6

Genesis 4:6-7 ESV
"(6) The LORD said to Cain, 'Why are you angry, and why has your face fallen? (7) If you do well, will you not be accepted? And if you do not do well, sin is crouching at the door. Its desire is for you, but you must rule over it.'"

There is a profound truth here that we seem to overlook when the Lord corrects Cain for bringing an offering that was unacceptable. If you choose to walk in areas away from the things of the Lord, "sin is crouching at the door". The picture is that of some vicious animal just waiting for someone to open the door just a little bit and it will enter and attack. Most of the time when sin presents itself we fail to see its destructive power over us, but instead see it only as something to play with, to entertain and to yield to its power. Maybe if we saw sin for what it really is, we would be more cautious to rule over it. Jesus says in John 10:10 *"The thief cometh not, but for to steal, and to kill, and to destroy: I am come that they might have life, and that they might have it more abundantly."*

Add your thoughts and/or prayer for the day

January 3
Genesis 7-9

Genesis 9:13
"I do set my bow in the cloud, and it shall be for a token of a covenant between me and the earth."

A rainbow is the Lord's signature to a covenant He has made with us. He gave that promise to Noah over 4,000 years ago, and He continues to this day to keep it. Every time we see a rainbow, it is God reminding us that He keeps His promises. The rainbow not only reminds us of God's faithfulness, but also His constant presence and watch care over us. The rain may come in our lives, but God will always find a way to bring a rainbow, a promise, His very presence as part of it. So if there is a storm in your life, just keep looking for the rainbow, God is with you and He is faithful to keep His promises.

Add your thoughts and/or prayer for the day

January 4
Genesis 10-12

Genesis 12:9-10
"(9) And Abram journeyed, going on still toward the south. (10) And there was a famine in the land: and Abram went down into Egypt to sojourn there; for the famine was grievous in the land."

Abraham had obeyed the Lord up until this point, going where the Lord told him, but when the circumstances changed and famine overtook the land God had promised him, he takes charge and goes on south to Egypt where trouble waited for him. Walking with the Lord does not always mean an easy journey. When the disciples asked Jesus about following Him, He replied that the Son of Man had no place to lay His head. This idea of thinking that God's will is the easy road or a materially prosperous road is not the truth. God wants us to be willing to trust Him by faith during times of famine or need. This is the place where faith is established and grown. When in difficult times don't look for the easy road. Instead stand still, trust in the Lord and don't you dare move until you are certain it is God's will for you!

Add your thoughts and/or prayer for the day

<u>January 5</u>
Genesis 13-15

Genesis 13:12-13
"(12) Abram dwelled in the land of Canaan, and Lot dwelled in the cities of the plain, and pitched his tent toward Sodom. (13) But the men of Sodom were wicked and sinners before the LORD exceedingly."

Genesis 14:12
"And they took Lot, Abram's brother's son, who dwelt in Sodom, and his goods, and departed."

Lot saw the well watered plains of Jordan and decided that it would be to his advantage to bring his family there without thinking of the consequences of his actions. At first he just 'pitched his tent toward Sodom' but it is not long before he is living 'in Sodom'. Listen up! If you begin by allowing the little things to slip by you, it won't be long until you have accepted them as being okay for you. You've seen this happen, maybe you're guilty of it today; a dad or mom will sleep in on Sunday or plan an activity away from church and before long they are missing church regularly and in the end they are praying for their grown children who never attend church and their grandchildren who are lost. We need to guard ourselves against Satan's tactics of warfare. He will just get you to pitch your tent toward sin thinking in some way it won't hurt you, but in the end the consequences will destroy you and your family.

<u>Add your thoughts and/or prayer for the day</u>

January 6
Genesis 16-18

Genesis 16:2
"And Sarai said unto Abram, Behold now, the LORD hath restrained me from bearing: I pray thee, go in unto my maid; it may be that I may obtain children by her. And Abram hearkened to the voice of Sarai."

God had promised Abraham a son in his old age, but Sarai had become impatient with the Lord's promise and had figured out a way to supposedly help the Lord out. Because of this they brought about a problem that would plague Israel the rest of history. God's word is true and can be trusted. He never fails on His promises, but the timing of His promises is His and His alone. We must be patient and trusting to receive God's best. Not only is His timing His; His promise is His and He doesn't need our help in fulfilling His promises. All He needs from us is faith in Him. When our faith wavers, is when we get ourselves into trouble trying to help God out. Be careful today in that thing that seems impossible. You are standing where God is working. Be still and wait for the promise of His involvement. He will not fail you!

Add your thoughts and/or prayer for the day

January 7
Genesis 19-21

Genesis 19:14
"So Lot went out and said to his sons-in-law, who were to marry his daughters, "Up! Get out of this place, for the LORD is about to destroy the city." But he seemed to his sons-in-law to be jesting."

Lot had left his uncle Abraham and had moved toward Sodom until finally he had brought his family into this sinful place and had been apparently consumed by its sinful culture. He even refers to the sinful men of Sodom as 'brethren' in verse 7. Now when God makes him aware of the destruction that is to come, he has no spiritual influence on the men who were to marry his daughters. Makes one wonder if we realize how important our spiritual witness is to those who will suffer an eternal punishment if they do not turn to God. Have we become so much a part of the worldly culture that when we speak of the things of God no one will take us seriously? Have we failed to be a spiritual influence for our children to the point that they will not see the importance of a godly mate? We must be on guard as how subtly the world will influence us away from the truth of God.

Add your thoughts and/or prayer for the day

January 8
Genesis 22-24

Genesis 24:31
"And he said, Come in, thou blessed of the LORD; wherefore standest thou without? for I have prepared the house, and room for the camels."

The servant of Abraham, not a family member but a servant is referred to as "thou blessed of the Lord" by Laban the brother of Rebecca. As you read the story you will find that this man had a true faith in the Lord, praying for guidance and continually worshipping the Lord at every opportunity and constantly referring to what the Lord had done in his journey. Wouldn't it be great if people would be able to recognize us as "blessed of the Lord" by our constant recognition of the Lord's involvement in our lives. Go ahead and pray in the presence of unbelievers, speak words of blessing when you are aware of God's activity, and worship Him constantly for His faithfulness to you. Some may call you crazy, but most will say you are blessed of the Lord.

Add your thoughts and/or prayer for the day

January 9
Genesis 25-27

Genesis 26:24
"And the LORD appeared unto him the same night, and said, I am the God of Abraham thy father: fear not, for I am with thee, and will bless thee, and multiply thy seed for my servant Abraham's sake."

The Lord tells Isaac that he will be blessed for his father's sake. What a thought, that our lives play such an important part in our children's lives. Just as we know from scripture that the sins of the father affect the lives of his children, here we see where the committed life of a father can and does bring blessing to his children. Maybe you were fortunate enough to have had a godly father and been given the opportunity to watch his life as he faithfully served the Lord, if so then thank God for your inheritance. But if you didn't, please don't let that keep you from being that kind of parent for your children. Remember this day, that your choices will have a direct impact on your sons and daughters. Thank God for dads who love and faithfully serve the Lord!

Add your thoughts and/or prayer for the day

January 10
Genesis 28-30

Genesis 28:20-21
*"(20) And Jacob vowed a vow, saying, If God will be with me,
and will keep me in this way that I go, and will give me bread
to eat, and raiment to put on, (21) So that I come again to
my father's house in peace; then shall the LORD be my God"*

Jacob is trying to 'cut a deal' with God. The problem here is that what Jacob is asking the Lord to do, the Lord had already promised Jacob he was going to do. Jacob had learned early on that to get what you want, you must be able to connive your way into a deal. It will take many years of God's involvement in his life to rid him of this character flaw. We don't make deals with God; we serve Him and obey Him. He is God and we are not! There is a heretical teaching being propagated by many preachers today that says you can demand God to do what you want and with enough faith, God will have to do what you say. Stop trying to manipulate God, it just won't work! Let God be god of your life, it will turn out far better than if you are in control.

Add your thoughts and/or prayer for the day

January 11
Genesis 31-33

Genesis 32:28-30
"(28) And he said, Thy name shall be called no more Jacob, but Israel: for as a prince hast thou power with God and with men, and hast prevailed. (29) And Jacob asked him, and said, Tell me, I pray thee, thy name. And he said, Wherefore is it that thou dost ask after my name? And he blessed him there. (30) And Jacob called the name of the place Peniel: for I have seen God face to face, and my life is preserved."

Jacob has been changed by the experiences he has had while serving Laban. Now it appears that every time he has an encounter with God, he leaves a memorial to remind him of that experience. Here he is left with more than just to name a place or to leave a pile of rocks as a reminder for he will walk with a limp the rest of his life. But even beyond that, the Lord gives him a new name, instead of Jacob which means 'deceiver' he will be called Israel which means 'he will rule as god'. When the Lord truly touches the life of a person, they will forever be changed. There may be some physical change, but most importantly they will not be the same person they were before. They will live with a divine purpose from that point on.

Add your thoughts and/or prayer for the day

January 12
Genesis 34-36

Genesis 35:2-3
"(2) Then Jacob said unto his household, and to all that were with him, Put away the strange gods that are among you, and be clean, and change your garments: (3) And let us arise, and go up to Bethel; and I will make there an altar unto God, who answered me in the day of my distress, and was with me in the way which I went."

Jacob had gotten side-tracked in returning to his father and as he had tarried from completing God's will as he had been directed, it led to his family becoming involved with a heathen people. Instead of their influencing the world to be godly, they had allowed the world to influence them toward false religion. How easily the world will influence us and our children if we refrain from walking day by day and hour by hour with the Lord. Guard yourself and your family from that which will in time destroy your relationship with the Lord.

Add your thoughts and/or prayer for the day

January 13
Genesis 37-39

Genesis 39:5-6
"(5) And it came to pass from the time that he had made him overseer in his house, and over all that he had, that the LORD blessed the Egyptian's house for Joseph's sake; and the blessing of the LORD was upon all that he had in the house, and in the field. (6) And he left all that he had in Joseph's hand; and he knew not ought he had, save the bread which he did eat. And Joseph was a goodly person, and well favoured."

Joseph was sold into slavery by his brothers to a foreign country that did not worship the one true God, but even in all this he was a godly man. If there was ever a character in scripture that seemingly had the right to question God for his circumstances it would be Joseph, yet what we find is that his faith in God's ability to work all things out to His favor was where Joseph found his strength and as a result God was able to bless him. Do you let your circumstances control your spirituality or do you let your love and faith in God direct you through the circumstances? Just remember that God is always working out His plan for your benefit.

Add your thoughts and/or prayer for the day

January 14
Genesis 40-42

Genesis 41:52
"The name of the second he called Ephraim, For God has made me fruitful in the land of my affliction."

Joseph naming his two children born to him in Egypt discloses a wonderful truth to how he viewed all his trials. In looking at all the trouble he had been through for those past several years from being sold by his brothers as a slave, being falsely accused by Potiphar's wife, being forgotten by the cupbearer and being a prisoner of Egypt; he now says God has made him fruitful in the land of his affliction. Paul taught with this same spirit when faced with an affliction that persisted no matter how he prayed for it to leave him, but then the Lord told him that His grace would be sufficient and Paul saw the affliction as a blessing of the Lord. How many times do we miss the blessing of our problems because we fail to see them as God's instruments for deliverance of His grace? Instead of complaining, we should be patient in our trials to see how the Lord might be using them in His timing to bring about a blessing we could not receive any other way.

Add your thoughts and/or prayer for the day

January 15
Genesis 43-45

Genesis 43:23
He replied, "Peace to you, do not be afraid. Your God and the God of your father has put treasure in your sacks for you. I received your money." Then he brought Simeon out to them.

This is the reply of the Egyptian steward of Joseph's house to the questioning of Joseph's brothers. It is interesting that in his answer would acknowledge the fact that all was done by *"your God and the God of your father"*. This man would have worshipped the gods of Egypt, but by his statement he knew the power of the one true God of Israel. It tells us a lot about Joseph's faithful witness of the Lord. Here he is the prince of Egypt, raised to power from the depths of prison to second in command of the whole country and still very much a witness of the one true God. Is it any wonder why the Lord had blessed him? It is said that the true character of a man is who he is when no one is watching him. In our plight to make a living and raise our children, we should be constantly aware of the fact that our true character is always on trial. Stay faithful; you never know how God is going to use your witness for His glory.

Add your thoughts and/or prayer for the day

January 16
Genesis 46-48

Genesis 48:20
"And he blessed them that day, saying, In thee shall Israel bless, saying, God make thee as Ephraim and as Manasseh: and he set Ephraim before Manasseh."

This is Jacob giving special blessing to his grandchildren. As parents we should understand the importance of blessings! In offering them our blessing, we are giving our children ownership to their part in the work of God through their lives. We spend a lot of time teaching our children how to succeed as part of society, but more important is making them heirs to their purpose as children of God. Use every opportunity to encourage your children to live out their purpose before the Lord.

Add your thoughts and/or prayer for the day

January 17
Genesis 49 - Exodus 1

Genesis 50:19-20
"(19) And Joseph said unto them, Fear not: for am I in the place of God? (20) But as for you, ye thought evil against me; but God meant it unto good, to bring to pass, as it is this day, to save much people alive."

The grace that Joseph shows his brothers is born out of his faith that God was in control of his life, not him. Even to his brothers he says that he would never try to take the place of God. Our problems stem from the desire to run our lives instead of letting God have His perfect work in and through us. Adam's sin was propagated when the serpent suggested that by eating the fruit, they would be as gods. The one true God is the only one who deserves to be God and you can trust that whatever He requires of you, it is only for your good, no matter how hard it may seem.

Add your thoughts and/or prayer for the day

January 18
Exodus 2-4

Exodus 3:10-12
"(10) Come now therefore, and I will send thee unto Pharaoh, that thou mayest bring forth my people the children of Israel out of Egypt. (11) And Moses said unto God, Who am I, that I should go unto Pharaoh, and that I should bring forth the children of Israel out of Egypt? (12) And he said, Certainly I will be with thee; and this shall be a token unto thee, that I have sent thee: When thou hast brought forth the people out of Egypt, ye shall serve God upon this mountain."

When we are convinced that God has called us to be a follower of His word, there is always a sense of inability. You see we know ourselves and we know how incapable we are as humans to react to the supernatural work of God because of how many times we have failed in the past. However, when God speaks to us His purpose, we should be reminded that He is the all-powerful, miracle-working, creator and sovereign Lord. What we can't do in and of ourselves, He can and will do through us as we allow ourselves to be controlled by Him. Die to self to be moved by the resurrection power of your Lord and see God do that which only He can do through you!

Add your thoughts and/or prayer for the day

January 19
Exodus 5-7

Exodus 7:4-5
"(4) But Pharaoh shall not hearken unto you, that I may lay my hand upon Egypt, and bring forth mine armies, and my people the children of Israel, out of the land of Egypt by great judgments. (5) And the Egyptians shall know that I am the LORD, when I stretch forth mine hand upon Egypt, and bring out the children of Israel from among them."

Some will ask why God required Moses to go back to Pharaoh so many times before the release of Israel from their bondage. First and foremost God wanted the Egyptians to know they were dealing with the one true God. Secondly, the Lord wanted Israel to witness His power because they were going to need to have faith that He could get them free from Egypt and into the Promised Land. And lastly, God was making a leader who would trust Him when the going got tough. As you read this story, you will find times when Moses will question God, but each time the Lord gives Moses just enough information to get him through. When God is working in our lives, He has the advantage of knowing the future and although we may question Him, we should learn to have faith in His power to accomplish what He wants and He will do what is necessary to care for us and give us what is best for us.

Add your thoughts and/or prayer for the day

January 20
Exodus 8-10

Exodus 9:15-16
"(15) For now I will stretch out my hand, that I may smite thee and thy people with pestilence; and thou shalt be cut off from the earth. (16) And in very deed for this cause have I raised thee up, for to shew in thee my power; and that my name may be declared throughout all the earth."

This was God's message to Pharaoh, an unsaved heathen dictator who was the most powerful man on earth at the time. Yet as powerful as he thought he was, he was no match for the God of the universe. God uses this man's hardened heart and continual refusals to demonstrate to the world, how powerful He is. Also with each time Moses had to go before Pharaoh, his confidence grew stronger as he knew God was greater than this man. We will find that each time God puts us to the test of facing our fears; we too, become bolder because we learn of God's omnipotent power. So no matter what or who you may fear, you should know that the God you serve is more powerful and nothing can happen to you that God is not aware of nor that He can use for His glory. Our God is an awesome God!

Add your thoughts and/or prayer for the day

Exodus 13:8
"And thou shalt shew thy son in that day, saying, 'This is done because of that which the LORD did unto me when I came forth out of Egypt.'"

The Israelites' redemption from their bondage in Egypt is symbolic to our being redeemed from our bondage to sin at salvation. When we consider this, God reminds us that our salvation story is an important one to be shared with our children. At every opportunity we as parents should be quick and consistent to share our testimony of how the Lord saved us, how He is a part of our lives, how He blesses us and how He answers our prayers. Dear child of God, it is your responsibility to raise up your child in the nurture and admonition of the Lord. Do not leave this to anyone else to do as God has appointed you to the task. Too many children have Christian parents who have yet to tell them of how they came to know the Lord, the most important information they could ever share. Don't wait! Do it today!

Add your thoughts and/or prayer for the day

January 22
Exodus 14-16

Exodus 14:13-14
"*(13) And Moses said unto the people, Fear ye not, stand still, and see the salvation of the LORD, which he will shew to you to day: for the Egyptians whom ye have seen to day, ye shall see them again no more for ever. (14) The LORD shall fight for you, and ye shall hold your peace.*"

Here the children of Israel felt trapped with the Red Sea on one side and the Egyptian army approaching from the other, there seemed no escape. The man of God stands in faith without knowing what God intended and told them to stand still, God was on His way. When we are in those situations that seem to have no answers, no escape, no hope, that is the time to be still, because God is about to reveal Himself in a way we have never experienced before. It requires our faith to stand strong enough to wait on Him, but if we will watch closely, the Lord will do that which only He can do. It may not be the deliverance we expected, but it will be God's presence in the storm that will give us the direction we need. You will never go wrong waiting on the Lord. Just be still!

Add your thoughts and/or prayer for the day

January 23
Exodus 17-19

Exodus 17:11-12
"(11) And it came to pass, when Moses held up his hand, that Israel prevailed: and when he let down his hand, Amalek prevailed. (12) But Moses' hands were heavy; and they took a stone, and put it under him, and he sat thereon; and Aaron and Hur stayed up his hands, the one on the one side, and the other on the other side; and his hands were steady until the going down of the sun."

God blesses a leader who will follow His command, but every godly leader realizes that he needs the help of others. The truth is that a man who thinks he should lead alone is either very foolish or very prideful, both of which will not honor the Lord. What is your role in leadership? Whether it is supporting the hands of the leader or fighting the battles as he directs, everyone is important in the work of God. Consider those God has led into your life to provide you and your family with leadership; Do you support them when there is a need by helping as you can or do you leave it to them to fight alone?

Add your thoughts and/or prayer for the day

January 24
Exodus 20-22

Exodus 20:7
*"Thou shalt not take the name of the LORD thy God in vain;
for the LORD will not hold him guiltless that taketh his name
in vain."*

One of the ten commandments of the Lord is used as a proof text for not using the Lord's name as a curse word and certainly we should not do that at all. But there is more to this command than just a slip of the tongue; to all those who have claimed to be a child of God, you have taken His name as your identity. Much like you are known by your last name to be a part of your family, you have been given the Lord's name as you were adopted into His family. So dear child of God, you must understand that your actions either bring honor or dishonor to the family name. If you are a child of God and fail to live in a way that honors the name of God then you have taken the name of the Lord in vain. Now that opens up a whole new idea to this command. Your life should be a constant witness of whose child you are!

Add your thoughts and/or prayer for the day

January 25
Exodus 23-25

Exodus 23:30-31 ESV
"(30) Little by little I will drive them out from before you, until you have increased and possess the land. (31) And I will set your border from the Red Sea to the Sea of the Philistines, and from the wilderness to the Euphrates, for I will give the inhabitants of the land into your hand, and you shall drive them out before you."

The Lord describes how He will give the Promised Land to Israel. Note He says 'little by little' until they have possessed all that He desires for them. That is how the Lord works in our lives in bringing us into the fullness of Christ. This is a lifetime of work; when we start this path we will stay on it until we are glorified when we enter our eternal home. Don't get impatient, but consider the area where the Lord is dealing with you today. Each time the Spirit is able to take ownership of an area of our lives we become more like our Savior. No matter how large or small, God is working in us desiring to conform us to the image of His Son. Remember, God won't waste using anything in your life for His benefit!

Add your thoughts and/or prayer for the day

January 26
Exodus 26-28

Exodus 28:34-35
"(34) A golden bell and a pomegranate, a golden bell and a pomegranate, upon the hem of the robe round about. (35) And it shall be upon Aaron to minister: and his sound shall be heard when he goeth in unto the holy place before the LORD, and when he cometh out, that he die not."

The reading this morning is of the intricate details of the tabernacle and the priest's robe. The Lord was so specific down to the last detail. In setting up the worship of the tabernacle, priests and people it is clear that it was to be done in a holy reverence, in a divine order and in honor of who He is. Today's so-called worship many times is anything but holy, reverent, or divine. It will bring honor more to the performers of so called worship than the One to whom the worship is supposedly given. When the Lord established congregational worship, He was specific in its order. We might do well to make sure our worship is to Him and not for ourselves.

Add your thoughts and/or prayer for the day

January 27
Exodus 29-31

Exodus 29:36
"And every day you shall offer a bull as a sin offering for atonement. Also you shall purify the altar, when you make atonement for it, and shall anoint it to consecrate it."

The Lord required blood for everything that was to be consecrated to Him and to His service. He also required blood offerings every day for a sin offering. From the very beginning when Adam sinned, the Lord made them coverings of skin meaning that a innocent sacrifice was made in order to cover their sin. Throughout the scriptures, the Lord is clear that without the shedding of blood there would be no forgiveness of sin. When Jesus came, He came as the Lamb of God sent to be our blood offering, a sacrifice for our sins once and for all as He was sacrificed on Calvary. It is through His atonement for our sin that we can find access to the Holy God and become a child of God. Consider Him today, for without His shed blood we would have no salvation.

Add your thoughts and/or prayer for the day

January 28
Exodus 32-34

Exodus 32:9-11
"(9) And the LORD said unto Moses, 'I have seen this people, and, behold, it is a stiffnecked people: (10) Now therefore let me alone, that my wrath may wax hot against them, and that I may consume them: and I will make of thee a great nation.' (11) And Moses besought the LORD his God, and said, 'LORD, why doth thy wrath wax hot against thy people, which thou hast brought forth out of the land of Egypt with great power, and with a mighty hand?'"

Exodus 32:14
"And the LORD repented of the evil which he thought to do unto his people."

Some have struggled with this passage in thinking that in some way Moses had power to change the mind of God. In this dialogue between God and man, we actually see the grace of God being demonstrated, not the power of man over God's sovereignty. Did Moses really change the mind of God? No more than you did when you received His grace and in doing so, were turned from a hell bound sinner into a heaven-bound child of God. God's judgment on sin is a righteous judgment and if carried out, would end in God's wrath consuming all of us, but through His grace we obtain salvation that gives us eternal acceptance and forgiveness instead of the wrath and judgment we deserve.

Add your thoughts and/or prayer for the day

January 29
Exodus 35-37

Exodus 36:5-6
"(5) *And they spake unto Moses, saying, 'The people bring much more than enough for the service of the work, which the LORD commanded to make.' (6) And Moses gave commandment, and they caused it to be proclaimed throughout the camp, saying, 'Let neither man nor woman make any more work for the offering of the sanctuary.' So the people were restrained from bringing.*"

The people who had been given the opportunity to give to the work of building the tabernacle were so excited and so generous with their giving that Moses had to command them to stop because they had more than enough for the work. When God is moving in a place to accomplish His will, we too should realize the importance of the work and get excited at the opportunity He has given us to be a part of His work either by giving our offerings or by giving ourselves to the work. It seems so much of the time, preachers are begging for help with the work, with little if any real excitement to get involved. We might want to check our availability and desire when it comes to the Lord's work compared to what we offer to activities that do not have such an eternal value.

Add your thoughts and/or prayer for the day

January 30
Exodus 38-40

Exodus 40:16
"Thus did Moses: according to all that the LORD commanded him, so did he."

The phrase, 'as the Lord commanded Moses' appears thirteen times in the last two chapters of Exodus. One thing we see of Moses is that he always went to the Lord for direction. No wonder he was the greatest leader in the history of Israel. God can do great things, but He always uses the instrument of man. The reason we don't see as much of what God can do is because man is too busy doing his own thing, instead of as the Lord commands him. In our personal lives, homes, churches and nation, man has forgotten to seek the Lord and then do what He says and the result is that our world has yet to see the true power and might of our God. The challenge today is that it be said of us that we live as the Lord commands us.

Add your thoughts and/or prayer for the day

January 31
Leviticus 1-3

Leviticus 1:4
"He shall lay his hand on the head of the burnt offering, and it shall be accepted for him to make atonement for him."

At the close of Exodus, God has provided a place for worship and now in Leviticus, He will give instruction for worship. One of the greatest attributes of true worship is the acknowledgement of God providing an atonement for our sin. Before Christ, this was signified by the sinner laying his hands upon the head of the sacrifice symbolizing the substitutionary act of the sacrifice becoming sin for him. Because of our sinful condition, we have no way to atone for our own sins; we need someone to be an atonement for us, someone innocent of sin who could take our place. We have the supreme substitutionary sacrifice in Jesus who became sin for us. The atonement for our sin is through Christ, not through our own good works because we have none (Isaiah 64:6).

Add your thoughts and/or prayer for the day

February 1
Leviticus 4-6

Leviticus 5:17 ESV
"If anyone sins, doing any of the things that by the LORD's commandments ought not to be done, though he did not know it, then realizes his guilt, he shall bear his iniquity."

Living in California for a time, I had once loaded the kids up in the back of the truck and was going to the store. I hadn't gone far until a policeman pulled me over and I was cited for violating the law by allowing the children to ride in the back of the truck. I argued that I grew up in Texas and we always rode in the back of the truck. To which the officer responded that ignorance of the law does not excuse our responsibility to the law. I got a ticket and had to pay that fine. The same is true of God's law. When we have violated His law, we are responsible for bearing the guilt of our sin when we are made aware of it. It is no time to find blame or try in any way to excuse ourselves; it is time to get things right with the Lord! Harboring sin only hinders our fellowship with the Lord, and that never pays well to our benefit.

Add your thoughts and/or prayer for the day

February 2
Leviticus 7-9

Leviticus 8:23
"And he slew it; and Moses took of the blood of it, and put it upon the tip of Aaron's right ear, and upon the thumb of his right hand, and upon the great toe of his right foot."

At the ordination of the priesthood of Aaron, Moses takes the blood of the ram and puts it on the lobe of the ear, the thumb and the toe. The symbolism is that the blood-tipped ear speaks of the ear that will hear the voice of God. One who serves the Lord must be listening to the voice of God. The natural man does not receive or understand the things of Christ. The blood-tipped thumb symbolizes the hand that was essential for service. There is an active part to a person who will serve the Lord that requires he be involved. And the blood-tipped toe symbolizes that it is essential for the walk to remain consecrated before Lord. To be an honest servant of the Lord, one must be totally surrendered to hear, act and move by the Lord's commands.

Add your thoughts and/or prayer for the day

February 3
Leviticus 10-12

Leviticus 11:45
"For I am the LORD that bringeth you up out of the land of Egypt, to be your God: ye shall therefore be holy, for I am holy."

In all the laws that were being established, God's desire for His people was that they be different from the world, to desire to be like Him, to love holiness, to live as the redeemed. How disrespecting and dishonoring for His children who experience His forgiveness, love and protection to live any other way. God is calling us daily to live in holiness, living up to the calling He has put upon us by calling us His children. Live today as a true child of God ... be like your Father!

Add your thoughts and/or prayer for the day

February 4
Leviticus 13-16

Leviticus 16:34
"'And this shall be an everlasting statute unto you, to make an atonement for the children of Israel for all their sins once a year.' And he did as the LORD commanded Moses."

Packed into the laws for cleansing is this one day that the Lord sets apart as the Day of Atonement. God establishes a way in which Israel will have their sins atoned by the blood of a sacrifice administered by the high priest. All of this points to the supreme sacrifice of Jesus Christ, administered for us by the resurrected high priest, Jesus, who in Himself provides the sacrifice, the work of the priest, the scapegoat and the continual and eternal atonement for our sin. *"O what a Savior, O hallelujah, His heart was broken on Calvary, His hands were nail-scarred, His side was riven, He gave His life-blood for even me."*

Add your thoughts and/or prayer for the day

February 5
Leviticus 17-20

Leviticus 18:3-4 ESV
"(3) *You shall not do as they do in the land of Egypt, where you lived, and you shall not do as they do in the land of Canaan, to which I am bringing you. You shall not walk in their statutes. (4) You shall follow my rules and keep my statutes and walk in them. I am the LORD your God.*"

God was calling out Israel to be different from the world, just as he calls us out to live separated from the world. So many who take the name of Christ as being Christians are allowing themselves to be pulled back into the world they were saved from. The traditions and philosophies of men are being their guides instead of the Word of God. It is getting harder to tell the Christian from the non-Christian because the Christian is being influenced by the world instead of the world being influenced by the Christian. Even in our churches, the attitudes, the dress, the music, and even the preaching have taken on a flavor of the world. Is your Christianity influencing the world or have you been more influenced by the world? A question we must answer and then be resolved to live as a child of God.

Add your thoughts and/or prayer for the day

February 6
Leviticus 21-24

Leviticus 24:16
*"And he that blasphemeth the name of the LORD, he shall
surely be put to death, and all the congregation shall
certainly stone him: as well the stranger, as he that
is born in the land, when he blasphemeth the
name of the LORD, shall be put to death."*

It would seem that the Lord is very serious about how His name is to be used. God is holy and His name is holy, not to be used in any way that would discredit His holiness. Today, we can't go anywhere that we don't hear the world blaspheming the name of the Lord. Sadly, it is not just the world that dishonors our Savior; it is those that claim Him as their Lord as well. What is wrong in honoring God with our lips, upholding His holy nature by speaking with grace instead of cursing? Let us be like David who said in Psalms 19:14 *"Let the words of my mouth, and the meditation of my heart, be acceptable in thy sight, O LORD, my strength, and my redeemer."* If you are truly a child of God, watch your mouth!

Add your thoughts and/or prayer for the day

February 7
Leviticus 25-27

Leviticus 27:30
"And all the tithe of the land, whether of the seed of the land, or of the fruit of the tree, is the LORD'S: it is holy unto the LORD."

In all that the Lord requires a man do by the law, this 'tithe' seems to be important. He explains that the tithe is the first tenth of all that God gives a man and He is very specific that it 'is the Lord's: it is holy unto the Lord'. In all that we have; in all that God has given to us, it would appear that we should be very careful to honor Him by the first tenth of it by using it for Him or giving it to Him. Never consider what you have as yours, it is only yours as God has given it to you. Honor the Lord by the way you use it!

Add your thoughts and/or prayer for the day

February 8
Numbers 1-3

Numbers 3:12
"And I, behold, I have taken the Levites from among the children of Israel instead of all the firstborn that openeth the matrix among the children of Israel: therefore the Levites shall be mine;"

It is interesting that in the numbering of the people God did not allow Moses to number the Levites and here in this verse God declares them to be His. He makes a difference between the Israelites and the Levites. The Levites were to be His special servants to minister at the Tabernacle. A true pastor has been called or put into ministry by the Lord, not by some whim or desire. Their calling is one of responsibility to be true to the Word of God. They are always special and are to be treated with special care because they are the Lord's special servants. Take care of your man of God.

Add your thoughts and/or prayer for the day

February 9
Numbers 4-6

Numbers 6:24-26
*"(24) The LORD bless thee, and keep thee: (25) The LORD
make his face shine upon thee, and be gracious unto thee:
(26) The LORD lift up his countenance upon thee, and give
thee peace."*

The Lord had issued His plans and commissioned His work for each of the tribes of Israel. They are now prepared to move in His order into the promise land. As a conclusion to these commands and all has been set in place, God gives this blessing. In everything we see that He has a divine order. God loves order, and when His order is kept, we can be sure that these blessings will follow. He will preserve us, keep us, look upon us, be gracious to us, be present with us and give us His peace. What a promise! What a blessing! Has God commissioned you in some way to accompany Him in His work? If so, do it and reap the blessings He has for you.

Add your thoughts and/or prayer for the day

February 10
Numbers 7-9

Numbers 9:15
"And on the day that the tabernacle was reared up the cloud covered the tabernacle, namely, the tent of the testimony: and at even there was upon the tabernacle as it were the appearance of fire, until the morning."

The children of Israel had the tabernacle and a permanent representation of the presence of the Lord with a cloud by day and a pillar of fire by night. By these two symbols of God's presence they knew when to move and when to stay, where to go and where to stop. As New Testament believers, we have something far greater than they did, in that we have the indwelling Holy Spirit who is given to us at the point of salvation and is our individual guide. He guides us into all truth. He confirms our salvation and our relationship with the Father. He seals us, fills us, and empowers us. God dealt with Israel as a nation, but now the Lord deals with us personally. Oh, what an awesome God we serve! Oh, what a loving Father we have!

Add your thoughts and/or prayer for the day

February 11
Numbers 10-12

Numbers 11:21-23
"(21) *And Moses said, The people, among whom I am, are six hundred thousand footmen; and thou hast said, I will give them flesh, that they may eat a whole month. (22) Shall the flocks and the herds be slain for them, to suffice them? or shall all the fish of the sea be gathered together for them, to suffice them? (23) And the LORD said unto Moses, Is the LORD'S hand waxed short? thou shalt see now whether my word shall come to pass unto thee or not.*"

After the people's complaint for meat, the Lord tells Moses He will provide them with more meat than they will be able to consume. So Moses thinks that God's promise would require him to come up with the plan to do it and the Lord reminds Moses that He has the ability to do this without Moses' help. When the Lord is working His plan, it is our job to assist Him, not take over! Even in our assisting Him, we should always be reminded that it is His plan, to be carried out His way, to get His results! It is when we think we have a better plan that gets us in trouble.

Add your thoughts and/or prayer for the day

February 12
Numbers 13-15

Numbers 13:33
"And there we saw the giants, the sons of Anak, which come of the giants: and we were in our own sight as grasshoppers, and so we were in their sight."

The men of Israel that were sent to spy out the land God had promised them came back with this report. Instead of seeing the promise of God as big enough to defend them, they only saw an enemy big enough to defeat them. How many times have we failed to receive the blessings of seeing our God do that which only He can do because we were intimidated by the enemies of God? God is always bigger than our problems; however, His way of dealing with it may be different than what we would expect. Whatever you are facing today, look at it through eyes of faith and instead of seeing big problems see your awesome Lord, the King of kings and Lord of lords, Creator and Master of the universe! He is big enough and He loves you enough to see you through this!

Add your thoughts and/or prayer for the day

Numbers 16:3
"And they gathered themselves together against Moses and against Aaron, and said unto them, 'Ye take too much upon you, seeing all the congregation are holy, every one of them, and the LORD is among them: wherefore then lift ye up yourselves above the congregation of the LORD?'"

This is one of those chapters in scripture that exposes the importance of God's choice and God's positioning of people in responsibility. The Lord establishes leadership and expects there to be obedience to His leadership through them, whether it be the head of the house, the leaders in government, or the leadership in the church. These men had decided that they did not like the Lord's appointment of Moses and Aaron to give them leadership and challenged it, thinking that anyone could and should be leaders. The Lord caused the earth to open and swallow them up, because they had this attitude. Be careful with your challenging of God's leadership. He is very serious about whom He has chosen to lead and He will stand with them against you if He must. (Ephesians 5:22-23; Romans 13:1-2; Hebrews 13:17)

Add your thoughts and/or prayer for the day

Numbers 20:3-4
*"(3) And the people chode with Moses, and spake, saying,
'Would God that we had died when our brethren died before
the LORD! (4) And why have ye brought up the
congregation of the LORD into this wilderness,
that we and our cattle should die there?'"*

This is the people that had the chance to go into the promise land but refused to believe God and as a result were sent into the wilderness. Now as they are watching people die because of their disobedience, they want to blame Moses for their situation. How many times do we hear God being blamed for the ills of this world, when it is our fault, our sin that has brought on the disease, pain and suffering that we endure? God's intent for man was to live in a garden with everything provided for him, never to be sick, never to face death, but we chose to do things our way and still do. Instead of blaming God, we should be praising Him that He still loves us enough to want to save us.

Add your thoughts and/or prayer for the day

February 15
Numbers 22-24

Numbers 22:31-33
"(31) *Then the LORD opened the eyes of Balaam, and he saw the angel of the LORD standing in the way, with his drawn sword in his hand. And he bowed down and fell on his face. (32) And the angel of the LORD said to him, 'Why have you struck your donkey these three times? Behold, I have come out to oppose you because your way is perverse before me. (33) The donkey saw me and turned aside before me these three times. If she had not turned aside from me, surely just now I would have killed you and let her live.'"*

Balaam's donkey refused to go against the angel of the Lord, and yet Balaam could not see how God was trying to protect him through what Balaam thought was the stubbornness of the donkey. Oh, how many times it frustrates us to have something interrupt our schedule or stand in the way of something we want. Could it be that those interruptions might be the hand of God in some way protecting us from evil? Maybe instead of complaining we should be offering up thanksgiving to what God sees that we do not and accept by faith that the Father really does know what is best for us.

Add your thoughts and/or prayer for the day

February 16
Numbers 25-27

Numbers 25:1-3
"(1) And Israel abode in Shittim, and the people began to commit whoredom with the daughters of Moab. (2) And they called the people unto the sacrifices of their gods: and the people did eat, and bowed down to their gods. (3) And Israel joined himself unto Baalpeor: and the anger of the LORD was kindled against Israel."

The Lord had commanded Israel to stay pure from the other nations because He knew that in forming alliances with them, they would be drawn away into idol worship. God's desire for our purity is many times thwarted because we begin to find it comfortable to be in the world forming friendships and alliances with those who oppose our God. We may do this with the hope of influencing them for Christ's sake, but all too often their influence is greater than ours and we find ourselves doing things we never thought we would do. Don't lose your witness at the cost of friendship or peer pressure. God has called you to walk on higher ground.

Add your thoughts and/or prayer for the day

Numbers 30:2
"If a man vow a vow unto the LORD, or swear an oath to bind his soul with a bond; he shall not break his word, he shall do according to all that proceedeth out of his mouth."

God takes very seriously vows and promises because He will always keep His promises to us. He expects that when we promise Him something, that we will be like Him in keeping it. Today, our word or our promises don't seem to carry any weight. We have exchanged integrity for insincerity. Husbands and wives covenant with God to love each other the rest of their lives, but the promise is quickly broken at the first sign of any trouble. We make commitment to be faithful to the Lord with our offerings, but the first thing we cut when faced with financial difficulty is the Lord's offering. We make promises to our different relationships, yet fail to keep them. It is time that we become people of integrity and be known as someone who keeps our promises!

Add your thoughts and/or prayer for the day

Numbers 32:6-7
"(6) But Moses said to the people of Gad and to the people of Reuben, 'Shall your brothers go to the war while you sit here? (7) Why will you discourage the heart of the people of Israel from going over into the land that the LORD has given them?'"

The tribes of Reuben and Gad had decided they wanted to go ahead and settle for a land that was not part of the promised land, and when they approached Moses with the offer, his reply was *"shall your brothers go to war while you sit here?"* How many times in church work do we see the lack of interest by the whole while a few will wind up doing the work? It really is discouraging to those who will make the effort to help to not be backed up by those who sit on the sidelines. We know not everyone can physically do the work, but there is something everyone can do and that is to be an encouragement and support for those that can. How many times have you chosen to sit on the sidelines and do nothing simply because it was too much of an effort and you figured someone else could do it? Don't miss God's blessings for you, get in the game!

Add your thoughts and/or prayer for the day

February 19
Numbers 34-36

Numbers 36:13
"These are the commandments and the judgments, which the LORD commanded by the hand of Moses unto the children of Israel in the plains of Moab by Jordan near Jericho."

The Lord made sure that He had established the laws for the children of Israel, so there would be no question when it came time to disburse the lands and cities in the Promised Land. God's word is here to give us instruction for life. For some, they see God's word as restrictive, but God's intent is to provide guidelines so we could experience His best! Living in obedience to His word gives us the certainty that we have a life that will experience His very best.

Add your thoughts and/or prayer for the day

February 20
Deuteronomy 1-3

Deuteronomy 3:22
"Ye shall not fear them: for the LORD your God he shall fight for you."

As the children of Israel were approaching the Promised Land, God reassures them of His presence and power over their enemies. When God is directing us to a fuller, more committed life with Him, although there will be struggles to get there, we can be sure that He will go before us and aid us against the enemy that will try to oppose us having the victorious Christian life. Don't lose heart and do not give up! Jesus promised to give you life and give it more abundantly, so now go in and possess it!

Add your thoughts and/or prayer for the day

February 21
Deuteronomy 4-6

Deuteronomy 5:29
"O that there were such an heart in them, that they would fear me, and keep all my commandments always, that it might be well with them, and with their children forever!"

Do you hear the heart of a father desiring his children just love him enough to obey him? If you have been involved in raising children, you know the anguish that God was feeling when He made this statement. The Lord desires that we reverence Him in every area of our lives, conscious of the truth of His word and that by keeping His commandments, we would be able to influence our children to do the same. If you want the best for your kids, it can't be bought with money; it is given by a life committed to the Father who loves you.

Add your thoughts and/or prayer for the day

February 22
Deuteronomy 7-9

Deuteronomy 8:17-18
"(17) Beware lest you say in your heart, 'My power and the might of my hand have gotten me this wealth.' (18) You shall remember the LORD your God, for it is he who gives you power to get wealth, that he may confirm his covenant that he swore to your fathers, as it is this day."

There are so many who will claim that they are "self-made" successes, but the truth is that no one can make that claim! God is our creator and our sustainer and without His involvement in any of our lives, believer or non-believer, we could not even take our next breath, have our next thought, or take another step! Before we get high and mighty about claiming ourselves as some sort of success, it would do us well to remember who the true "High and Mighty" is and bow before him in humility and contrition that we would even begin to think of ourselves as something at all. Remember that it is the Lord who empowers us to accomplish the things we do and if anything we should stop often and thank Him for all that He has done for us and through us.

Add your thoughts and/or prayer for the day

February 23
Deuteronomy 10-12

Deuteronomy 11:26-28
*"(26) Behold, I set before you this day a blessing and a curse;
(27) A blessing, if ye obey the commandments of the LORD
your God, which I command you this day: (28) And a curse,
if ye will not obey the commandments of the LORD your God,
but turn aside out of the way which I command you this day,
to go after other gods, which ye have not known."*

The Lord lays out very clearly what He wants and what He will do in return for Israel's obedience, but He also explains in the same detail what the result will be if they choose to disobey. We too have a choice and just as with Israel, there are consequences that come with our choices. The commands of God are clear as well as His promise for the result of our obedience. As Joshua said, *"Choose you this day whom you will serve."* Just know there will always be consequences for your choices. Choose wisely, choose to obey!

Add your thoughts and/or prayer for the day

February 24
Deuteronomy 13-15

Deuteronomy 13:1-3 ESV
"(1) If a prophet or a dreamer of dreams arises among you and gives you a sign or a wonder, (2) and the sign or wonder that he tells you comes to pass, and if he says, 'Let us go after other gods,' which you have not known, 'and let us serve them,' (3) you shall not listen to the words of that prophet or that dreamer of dreams. For the LORD your God is testing you, to know whether you love the LORD your God with all your heart and with all your soul."

You may hear the argument concerning some of today's false teachers, that they have big churches or that they are healing people or some other "sign or wonder", so they must be men of God. Just because something or someone looks and sounds good, does not mean that they are something we as Christians should follow. Make your commitment to walk close to the Lord, keep His word dear to your heart. Then when that false teacher comes, you will be able to discern his false teaching. We are in the last days and there are a host of false teachers out there so don't be lured away into their false teaching by their charismatic character. Beware!

Add your thoughts and/or prayer for the day

February 25
Deuteronomy 16-18

Deuteronomy 16:17
"Every man shall give as he is able, according to the blessing of the LORD your God that he has given you."

The Lord is specific in what He requires of our giving. It is to be given first. It is to be our best. It is to be given at special times. It is to be given with a right heart attitude. Yet it seems that this one discipline for a Christian is the hardest for most. Here, the Lord just says to give according to the blessing the Lord has given us. So if you can't see where God has blessed you, then go ahead and be as stingy as you think God has been to you. But if you see the overwhelming blessings that God has blessed you with life, family, friends, job, health, and abilities to enjoy yourself, then give in the same abundance as you have received.

Add your thoughts and/or prayer for the day

February 26
Deuteronomy 19-21

Deuteronomy 20:3-4
"(3) ...today you are drawing near for battle against your enemies: let not your heart faint. Do not fear or panic or be in dread of them, (4) for the LORD your God is he who goes with you to fight for you against your enemies, to give you the victory.'

Just as with Israel, we are God's children who have received the Lord as our Savior and God has promised to be with us and empower us. When you face your enemies today, do not forget who stands beside you and is in you. Sometimes we forget that God does not allow anything in our lives that He does not plan to use for our good. So as you face those difficulties today, the Lord has not permitted these to come against you for your destruction, but for your edification and His glory. Give the Lord everything in this fight, let Him empower you and give you the wisdom needed and there will be victory in it for Him. However, if you decide to fight this in your own strength and understanding, the results will not be in your favor or His blessing.

Add your thoughts and/or prayer for the day

February 27
Deuteronomy 22-24

Deuteronomy 23:14
"Because the LORD your God walks in the midst of your camp, to deliver you and to give up your enemies before you, therefore your camp must be holy, so that he may not see anything indecent among you and turn away from you."

We should never forget that the Lord walks in the midst of our camp. That means He is in your business! We want Him to bless what we do, but if we are not careful of how we handle ourselves and our business, He will leave us to our own devices. If we are the children of the Lord, then we should walk in integrity, making sure that the activities of our life are those that will honor our Lord and Master. As the apostle Paul warns us we should walk *'circumspectly'* meaning that we are always aware of the things going on around us. Let's take care of our camp. It might do us well to spend a little time in our camp, doing a little house cleaning today.

Add your thoughts and/or prayer for the day

February 28
Deuteronomy 25-27

Deuteronomy 26:16-17
"(16) This day the LORD your God commands you to do these statutes and rules. You shall therefore be careful to do them with all your heart and with all your soul. (17) You have declared today that the LORD is your God, and that you will walk in his ways, and keep his statutes and his commandments and his rules, and will obey his voice."

The reading this morning listed a lot of laws that to us will seem unusual, but the reason for most of these laws was God's protection for the purity and the legacy of Israel. The Lord Jesus, when asked of the law, made it very simple; Love God with all your heart and love people as yourself. He said in doing this we would be obeying all the law. God wants us as His children to be obedient to Him, not that we in any way can be justified by our obedience, but that in doing so we are a testimony to the One who has provided our salvation by grace.

Add your thoughts and/or prayer for the day

March 1
Deuteronomy 28-30

Deuteronomy 30:16
"If you obey the commandments of the LORD your God that I command you today, by loving the LORD your God, by walking in his ways, and by keeping his commandments and his statutes and his rules, then you shall live and multiply, and the LORD your God will bless you in the land that you are entering to take possession of it."

What is the *'land that you are entering'*? It may be a time of suffering or a time of blessing. It may be an age of life or a new relationship. No matter where God has led you or what circumstance of life you have entered, it is God's desire that you take possession of it in accordance with His will and purpose. God does have a purpose for it! According to God's word, your victory in this place is found in remaining faithful to the His commands. So don't do this on your own, but seek out the Lord and His strength in the midst of it. If your heart remains faithful to Him, it is yours to possess!

Add your thoughts and/or prayer for the day

March 2
Deuteronomy 31-34

Deuteronomy 33:27
"The eternal God is your dwelling place, and underneath are the everlasting arms. And he thrust out the enemy before you and said, Destroy."

God has called us out to live in Him, to enjoy His protection and to be called His own. What an awesome act of grace that He has afforded to us, not because we deserve it, but because He chooses to love us! He even has offered us the victory over the enemy. He throws the enemy out before us and tells us to destroy. Isn't it strange that with all that God has done for us that when it comes to the enemy instead of destroying him we want to play with him? Doesn't make much sense now does it?

Add your thoughts and/or prayer for the day

March 3
Joshua 1-4

Joshua 2:11
"And as soon as we heard it, our hearts melted, and there was no spirit left in any man because of you, for the LORD your God, he is God in the heavens above and on the earth beneath."

Rahab's response to the spies who had come to spy out Jericho for Joshua gives us a hint as to the power of our testimony. She admitted that their knowledge of what God had done as the children of Israel had come across the wilderness had brought her to a place of belief in the one true God. Never underestimate the value of your personal story. When others see and hear what God has and is doing in our lives, it is a tool in the hand of the Spirit of God to reach the hearts of those who are unbelievers. Don't think you can't witness for Christ, just tell your story of your salvation and leave the rest to God! Share your testimony with someone this week.

Add your thoughts and/or prayer for the day

March 4
Joshua 5-7

Joshua 5:15
*"And the commander of the LORD's army said to Joshua,
"Take off your sandals from your feet, for the place where
you are standing is holy." And Joshua did so."*

Moses had been told this at the burning bush as God called him to lead the people of Israel, and now Joshua bows before Christ in the Promised Land just before a battle and is told the same. Any time we are facing a tough assignment that may seem above our pay grade, it is time to look to the Savior! These assignments are designed to accomplish His purposes and you can be sure that you are standing on holy ground. Your situation is bathed in the knowledge and grace of God. Just take your shoes off and bask in His power for the outcome.

Add your thoughts and/or prayer for the day

Joshua 9:14-15
"(14) And the men took of their victuals, and asked not counsel at the mouth of the LORD. (15) And Joshua made peace with them, and made a league with them, to let them live: and the princes of the congregation sware unto them."

After having some great victories, the men of Israel let their guard down. The enemy was able to disguise themselves and fool them into making a foolish covenant with them. Instead of continuing to depend solely on the Lord, they took it upon themselves to make decisions without consulting the Lord. As a result they would suffer for their decision the rest of their lives. How often we neglect the Lord's counsel and instead base our decisions on what we think would be best? It may take the time of seeking God's counsel and patiently waiting for the answer, but we best be careful to keep God in the loop! He has a much better vantage point from where He sits for making our life decisions.

Add your thoughts and/or prayer for the day

March 6
Joshua 11-14

Joshua 14:12
"Now therefore give me this mountain, whereof the LORD spake in that day; for thou heardest in that day how the Anakims were there, and that the cities were great and fenced: if so be the LORD will be with me, then I shall be able to drive them out, as the LORD said."

Caleb had been a faithful servant of God and after surviving the wilderness and helping settle the promise land, he now wants to claim his inheritance. It is a mountain full of giants instead a place that had already been captured and tamed, but he wanted that mountain. He had learned as we should, that we experience God's presence and power most when we are dependent on Him for our daily survival. Don't get too comfortable in your Christian walk; instead always look for that next mountain in your life where you will have God's help in clearing it out for His good.

Add your thoughts and/or prayer for the day

March 7
Joshua 15-18

Joshua 17:13
"Now when the people of Israel grew strong, they put the Canaanites to forced labor, but did not utterly drive them out."

How many times in our reading do we see that the Israelites took possession of the land, but did not utterly drive out the Canaanites? The Lord had promised them victory in the land, but they seemingly failed to live by that power. How many times in our lives have we taken hold of the possession of eternal life, been promised the abundant life in Christ, only to stop short of driving out the old man and all his carnal ways? If we are not experiencing the victorious and abundant life, it is probably because we have failed to empty ourselves of our carnal self. Drive out that old man and learn to live in the power of being "in Christ"; that old man is robbing you blind!

Add your thoughts and/or prayer for the day

March 8
Joshua 19-21

Joshua 21:45
"Not one word of all the good promises that the LORD had made to the house of Israel had failed; all came to pass."

What a testimony of the faithfulness of our Lord, to have kept every promise, not failing even once! You know He is still doing that; keeping His word, giving us all things out of His amazing grace! The Lord keeps His promises; that is for certain. He can do nothing less. Now comes the part that we may not like to consider; how many promises have we made and kept with Him? It seems so easy when things aren't going our way to find fault with Him, as if in some way He has failed to keep His promise to us, but the truth is that our failure to live according to His word is where the problems really lie. Do you keep your promises? He does!

Add your thoughts and/or prayer for the day

Joshua 24:14-15
"(14) *Now therefore fear the LORD, and serve him in sincerity and in truth: and put away the gods which your fathers served on the other side of the flood, and in Egypt; and serve ye the LORD. (15) And if it seem evil unto you to serve the LORD, choose you this day whom ye will serve; whether the gods which your fathers served that were on the other side of the flood, or the gods of the Amorites, in whose land ye dwell: but as for me and my house, we will serve the LORD.*"

After all that the Lord had done to deliver on His promise to give Israel the land of Canaan, who do you think they chose to serve? Well in truth they said they would serve the Lord, but in just a few short years they had turned their backs on Him once again. Sound familiar? Maybe that is why Joshua said it like he did; *"choose you this day whom you will serve".* You see, it is a daily choice that we must make in order to stay faithful to our Lord. So no matter the amount of times you may have failed in the past, the question is who will you serve today?

Add your thoughts and/or prayer for the day

Judges 2:10-11
"(10) And also all that generation were gathered unto their fathers: and there arose another generation after them, which knew not the LORD, nor yet the works which he had done for Israel. (11) And the children of Israel did evil in the sight of the LORD, and served Baalim:"

What a sad commentary on the parents who in just one generation, their children did not know the Lord or anything of the history that the Lord had done for them. It is just unbelievable that those who had experienced the victories and seen the hand of God move in such supernatural ways, would fail to tell their children of this awesome God. How can those who have tasted of the goodness of the Lord's salvation, His grace, His mercy and love, not make sure that their children have the same experience? It is not only unbelievable, it is heartless! If you are a parent, it is your responsibility to teach your children of your Lord and Savior. Do not leave this to anyone else to accomplish. Do it, and begin today!

Add your thoughts and/or prayer for the day

March 11
Judges 4-6

Judges 6:13
"And Gideon said unto him, Oh my Lord, if the LORD be with us, why then is all this befallen us? and where be all his miracles which our fathers told us of, saying, Did not the LORD bring us up from Egypt? but now the LORD hath forsaken us, and delivered us into the hands of the Midianites."

As the Lord approaches Gideon to call him to service, Gideon questions God's involvement with Israel being in bondage to the Midianites. Gideon had been told of all that God had done miraculously to save Israel in the past, but he had failed to learn of the disobedience of his people against God each time the Lord saved them. Today, many want to question God as to why we have illness, disasters, wars, and human failure. They look at God as if He owes us something, but the truth is that we owe Him for all He has done for us while the enemy continues to kill, steal and destroy. Look for God's miraculous hand in every situation, but understand the enemy will always cause havoc in order to get us to focus our attention away from the God of our salvation.

Add your thoughts and/or prayer for the day

March 12
Judges 7-9

Judges 7:2
"The LORD said to Gideon, "The people with you are too many for me to give the Midianites into their hand, lest Israel boast over me, saying, 'My own hand has saved me."

The story of Gideon and the 300-man army is one of God's ability to do so much with just a few who will follow Him. God will always choose to work in a way that demonstrates His glory over the glory of man. Yet He always chooses to use a man as a leader. Even Gideon who struggled with his faith, God uses in a mighty way to demonstrate His power and strength. God will operate among the least to do His greatest work, if only we will follow His commands.

Add your thoughts and/or prayer for the day

March 13
Judges 10-13

Judges 10:13-14
"(13) Yet ye have forsaken me, and served other gods: wherefore I will deliver you no more. (14) Go and cry unto the gods which ye have chosen; let them deliver you in the time of your tribulation."

When we finally realize we have gone as far as we can without God because we have messed our lives up to the point that there seems no hope, then we go crying for Him to pull us out. One day, like this that is described of Israel, the Lord will tell us to seek help from the gods we have been serving. As a nation, we have turned our backs on the one true God to serve the gods of government, humanitarianism, liberal ideology and we keep getting into a bigger mess. Don't be surprised when the Lord decides to leave us in this mess because we have refused to serve Him as the one true God.

Add your thoughts and/or prayer for the day

March 14
Judges 14-16

Judges 14:4
"But his father and his mother knew not that it was of the LORD, that he sought an occasion against the Philistines: for at that time the Philistines had dominion over Israel."

Samson was to be used by God to deliver Israel from the Philistines. Although his father and mother had been given assignment by the Lord as parents, they were unaware of all that God had planned. As you look into the eyes of a child, it would be good to remember that the calling upon the life of that child is of the Lord and our job is to do what He has commanded us as mentors and leave the outcome to the Lord. You just never know what your part is in the overall plan of God for that child. Be faithful, be an example and be spiritually sensitive.

Add your thoughts and/or prayer for the day

Judges 17:3
"And when he had restored the eleven hundred shekels of silver to his mother, his mother said, I had wholly dedicated the silver unto the LORD from my hand for my son, to make a graven image and a molten image: now therefore I will restore it unto thee."

Notice that the mother of Micah who *"wholly dedicated the silver unto the LORD",* would now use the silver to make an idol that would become an object of worship in the house of Micah her son. Today, many justify their misuse of the things of God by saying in some way they have dedicated it to the Lord. The Lord provides for us everything in order to live and we are to be good stewards of His blessings to us. How it must grieve the heart of God to see the very things He has given us for His worship being used to produce objects of worship that lead our children away from God instead of toward Him. Be careful if you carelessly consider the word of God as something you can just disregard if it doesn't fit your own desires, you may be establishing an idol that your children will worship instead of the one true God.

Add your thoughts and/or prayer for the day

March 16
Judges 20-21

Judges 21:25
"In those days there was no king in Israel: every man did that which was right in his own eyes."

When you read through these last few chapters of Judges, it is a mess for the people of Israel. There was wanton homosexuality, abuse of the women, hatred among the people, and although there were those who stood against this, many men of valor lost their lives defending godliness. All of this because they refused to listen to the Lord and instead did what was right in their own eyes. The Bible makes it very clear that man left to himself without God can and does make bad choices and creates only a mess of their lives. What is even worse is that their bad choices affect everyone else around them. The answer to the problem is to raise up godly children, win the lost and live by the word of God and all that begins with you.

Add your thoughts and/or prayer for the day

March 17
Ruth 1-2

Ruth 1:16
*"And Ruth said, Intreat me not to leave thee, or to return
from following after thee: for whither thou goest, I will go;
and where thou lodgest, I will lodge: thy people shall be my
people, and thy God my God:"*

The famous words of Ruth tell us something about Naomi. Although Naomi had followed her husband into Moab and allowed her sons to marry Moabite women against the will of God, she still had an impact as a witness for her one true God. Ruth had seen something in her mother-in-law that she did not see in others that would cause her to leave everything she had ever known and follow Naomi. When we are in the midst of unbelievers, we need to remember that our greatest witness is when we choose to follow the Lord in the midst of those who are lost. Jesus said that we should be salt and light in this world. No matter the circumstance, live up to your name, "child of God".

Add your thoughts and/or prayer for the day

March 18
Ruth 3-4

Ruth 3:12
"And now it is true that I am thy near kinsman: howbeit there is a kinsman nearer than I."

Boaz is a type of Christ and he tells Ruth that he would redeem her, but there was another kinsman that had to be dealt with first. The other redeemer is a type of the Law. As the story unfolds, we find that the other kinsman could not redeem Ruth because he would *'mar his own inheritance* (4:6). The only way the law could redeem would be for it to lower its standard to that of sinful man; it cannot because it would cease to be the law and the standard of God's righteousness. However, Jesus willingly takes on the responsibility to redeem us from sin paying the sin debt for us and giving us by grace His righteousness. If we are saved, we have been redeemed by the precious sacrifice of Jesus. Oh, how He loves you and me!

Add your thoughts and/or prayer for the day

1 Samuel 1:26-28
"(16) 'Sir,' Hannah said, 'a few years ago I stood here beside you and asked the LORD (27) to give me a child. Here he is! The LORD gave me just what I asked for. (28) Now I am giving him to the LORD, and he will be the LORD's servant for as long as he lives.' Elkanah worshiped the LORD there at Shiloh"

Two important issues we see here with Hannah; First that she kept her word to the Lord and secondly that as a mother she knew the importance of giving her child to the Lord. The psalmist tells us in Psalm 127:3 that our children are on loan to us from God and we are further instructed to raise them up to know Him. Moses wrote concerning God's word in Deuteronomy 6:7 *"And thou shalt teach them diligently unto thy children, and shalt talk of them when thou sittest in thine house, and when thou walkest by the way, and when thou liest down, and when thou risest up."* So many Christian parents seem to miss the boat on this one. That child that you so much love is the Lord's and it is your responsibility to give that child all the opportunities you can to make sure they will grow up to know and serve the Lord. Hanna also understood the importance of getting her son to the house of the Lord. Do you?

Add your thoughts and/or prayer for the day

March 20
1 Samuel 4-6

1 Samuel 4:3
"And when the people were come into the camp, the elders of Israel said, Wherefore hath the LORD smitten us to day before the Philistines? Let us fetch the ark of the covenant of the LORD out of Shiloh unto us, that, when it cometh among us, it may save us out of the hand of our enemies."

Israel had become so detached from a relationship with God that when they needed help they sought the things of God instead of God Himself. As a result, they lost the battle. Today people are wrapped up in all kinds of the things of God but fail in establishing and building their relationship with God. They have substituted music, emotional experiences, even certain kinds of preaching to satisfy what they deem as worship, but the truth is worship happens when we are intimate with our Lord. What do you look for when you want to feel close to the Lord? Be careful that you're not worshipping the things of God instead of God himself. That is where the victory is, in the Lord!

Add your thoughts and/or prayer for the day

March 21
1 Samuel 7-10

1 Samuel 8:19-20
"(19) Nevertheless the people refused to obey the voice of Samuel; and they said, Nay; but we will have a king over us; (20) That we also may be like all the nations; and that our king may judge us, and go out before us, and fight our battles."

Israel had it so good because God wanted to be their ruler, but all they could see was that they did not have a king like the other countries. Today the children of God are much the same, in that we have the very best that God wants to give us, yet all we see are the things the world has and think in some way God has kept something from us. Christians who spend their time chasing the things of the world find that those things leave them empty, unfulfilled, and usually in debt because they are not the things of our Lord. Be careful what you chase as entertainment or fulfillment, God has something so much better for you as His child.

Add your thoughts and/or prayer for the day

March 22
1 Samuel 11-13

1 Samuel 12:24-25
"(11) Only fear the LORD, and serve him in truth with all your heart: for consider how great things he hath done for you. (25) But if ye shall still do wickedly, ye shall be consumed, both ye and your king."

Samuel spoke these words to Israel reminding them of how good God had been to them as a nation, warning them that if they failed to live in obedience to the Lord, they would surely fall prey to God's chastisement. His warning would be well for us to remember as Americans. God has made our nation great as the generations before us honored Him and placed their trust in Him as He built and united us as a nation determined to live under God. But now we are falling headlong into a miry pit of humanism and liberal thought that leads us away from the foundational truths we were built upon. We would do well to heed the warning of Samuel that what God did to Israel, He could do to us.

Add your thoughts and/or prayer for the day

March 23
1 Samuel 14-16

1 Samuel 14:6
*"And Jonathan said to the young man that bare his armour,
Come, and let us go over unto the garrison of these
uncircumcised: it may be that the LORD will work
for us: for there is no restraint to the LORD
to save by many or by few."*

Jonathan understood something of God that so many fail to grasp. If God is in it (which He always is) then we can trust Him for the outcome, and it makes no difference if there is an apparent majority or not. You see, with God, size does not matter. In fact as we look through scripture we find that God loves to work with the least, in that He is glorified. He did it with Moses, Gideon, David, and Jonathan to name a few, and He will do it with you. Trust God when you feel outnumbered or too small for the task and watch the Lord do that which only He can do.

Add your thoughts and/or prayer for the day

March 24
1 Samuel 17-19

1 Samuel 17:45-46
"(45) Then said David to the Philistine, Thou comest to me with a sword, and with a spear, and with a shield: but I come to thee in the name of the LORD of hosts, the God of the armies of Israel, whom thou hast defied. (46) This day will the LORD deliver thee into mine hand; and I will smite thee, and take thine head from thee; and I will give the carcases of the host of the Philistines this day unto the fowls of the air, and to the wild beasts of the earth; that all the earth may know that there is a God in Israel."

The heart of a man of real faith is demonstrated in David as he faced Goliath. Without fear and with the resolve that God would be glorified through him, he stands against those who defy his God. Would that we be such men and women of faith, standing without fear but in complete faith, declaring our allegiance to the God who loves us, saved us and will empower us then trusting God for the outcome.

Add your thoughts and/or prayer for the day

March 25
1 Samuel 20-22

1 Samuel 20:32-33
"(32) And Jonathan answered Saul his father, and said unto him, Wherefore shall he be slain? what hath he done? (33) And Saul cast a javelin at him to smite him: whereby Jonathan knew that it was determined of his father to slay David."

Saul would have killed his own son in anger because he had become obsessed with jealousy toward David. It all started when David seemed to receive more honor than him after David killed Goliath. Jealousy is a wicked master. It will start with a simple ember of neglect or seeming disrespect, then it will play upon a person's every senses, blowing things out of proportion and finally taking control of our every action. To avoid this, the apostle Paul tells us to die to self. Promote others and not yourself.

Add your thoughts and/or prayer for the day

March 26
1 Samuel 23-25

1 Samuel 24:11-12
"(11) Moreover, my father, see, yea, see the skirt of thy robe in my hand: for in that I cut off the skirt of thy robe, and killed thee not, know thou and see that there is neither evil nor transgression in mine hand, and I have not sinned against thee; yet thou huntest my soul to take it. (12) The LORD judge between me and thee, and the LORD avenge me of thee: but mine hand shall not be upon thee."

David made a choice to honor King Saul instead of killing him. No doubt, no one would have blamed him had he killed Saul for all that he had done to destroy David, yet David would not harm him. Saul sought revenge while David sought restoration. One man is driven by pride and self while the other is driven by loyalty and a desire to serve. Every day we are called upon to make a choice in how we will respond to others. So will you be a Saul or will you be a David?

Add your thoughts and/or prayer for the day

March 27
1 Samuel 26-28

1 Samuel 28:18-19
"(18) *Because thou obeyedst not the voice of the LORD, nor executedst his fierce wrath upon Amalek, therefore hath the LORD done this thing unto thee this day. (19) Moreover the LORD will also deliver Israel with thee into the hand of the Philistines: and tomorrow shalt thou and thy sons be with me: the LORD also shall deliver the host of Israel into the hand of the Philistines.*"

God had made Saul king, had given him a man of God to be his counsel and yet when faced with the opportunity to be obedient, he chose instead to do things his own way and now he must suffer the consequences. There are always consequences for disobedience. We are foolish to think that in any way we can continue in sin and expect that in the end that God will in some way overlook our disobedience. The Lord has promised that He will chasten those He loves. It's not that he takes pleasure in the discipline He brings, but He desires a relationship that is built on love, loyalty, and honor. Seek to be obedient because of your love for the Father, not your fear of chastisement.

Add your thoughts and/or prayer for the day

March 28
1 Samuel 29-31

1 Samuel 30:18
"And David recovered all that the Amalekites had carried away: and David rescued his two wives."

God had commanded Saul to destroy the Amalekites, but he chose instead to do what he wanted. Because of it the Lord stripped his kingdom from him, and finally he is killed. But look who pops up to be an enemy against David and Judah, none other than the ones God had said to destroy. When we are brought to face our enemy, our sin, if we do not deal with it the way the Lord commands, we can be sure it will visit us again. Many times it will come with more power and more destruction than before. Just remember the sin you allow to fester in your life today will affect your life and the lives of your family in the future.

Add your thoughts and/or prayer for the day

March 29
2 Samuel 1-3

2 Samuel 3:17-18
"(17) And Abner had communication with the elders of Israel, saying, Ye sought for David in times past to be king over you: (18) Now then do it: for the LORD hath spoken of David, saying, By the hand of my servant David I will save my people Israel out of the hand of the Philistines, and out of the hand of all their enemies."

Abner refers to David as the servant of the Lord. David will be called the servant of the Lord some thirty times in the Old Testament. This was more than a title; it was David's heart toward the Lord. Over and over he inquires of the Lord about what he is to do or where he is to go and then the Lord responds, it reveals that he truly is a servant wanting to satisfy his Lord in these things. If we are to be a people after God's own heart, we too must learn to be servants of the Lord seeking out His direction and His desires for us before we take action. We have been called to the highest of callings --- to be a servant of Christ ---, but it is certainly one worth seeking.

Add your thoughts and/or prayer for the day

March 30
2 Samuel 4-6

2 Samuel 6:6-7
"(6) And when they came to Nachon's threshingfloor, Uzzah put forth his hand to the ark of God, and took hold of it; for the oxen shook it. (7) And the anger of the LORD was kindled against Uzzah; and God smote him there for his error; and there he died by the ark of God."

David and the people were doing what was right by returning the ark to Jerusalem, but they did it the wrong way. God had given very specific instruction on how the ark was to be handled. There are those who think as long as they are doing the Lord's work, it really doesn't matter how it is done. God is in the details, and if we are doing something in His name, we need to be very careful that it is done in His way. Just because something sounds good doesn't always mean that it is. Check with the instruction manual, the Bible.

Add your thoughts and/or prayer for the day

March 31
2 Samuel 7-9

2 Samuel 7:5-6
"(5) Go and tell my servant David, Thus saith the LORD, Shalt thou build me an house for me to dwell in? (6) Whereas I have not dwelt in any house (7) since the time that I brought up the (8) children of Israel out of Egypt, even (9) to this day, but have walked in a (10) tent and in a tabernacle."

David, after building himself a house to live in, decides that God needs such a house, but God speaks to Nathan and says no. God should not and cannot be contained in a house of our fixing. Too many people confine God conveniently in a box of their making, thinking they can in some way control His involvement in their lives. The only place God wants to dwell is in our hearts and even there, He is not to be constrained by our wills, but instead to do His will.

Add your thoughts and/or prayer for the day

April 1
2 Samuel 10-12

2 Samuel 12:13
"And David said unto Nathan, I have sinned against the LORD. And Nathan said unto David, The LORD also hath put away thy sin; thou shalt not die."

Such an important passage to consider as David had sinned and each time he tried to cover his sin, until finally he thinks he has gotten away with it. God sends Nathan the prophet to confront him with the word of God and David confesses his sin. Now notice what Nathan says; *"The LORD also hath put away thy sin; thou shalt not die"*. Do you realize that had David not repented at this point, it was God's intention to kill David? Sometimes we forget how our sin, hidden or not, breaks the heart of our Father. As a loving Father, He will not let us continue in sin without discipline, and if need be, He would call us home to protect His witness to others. If you are a child of God this is certainly something to think about as we choose whether to continue in sin or not.

Add your thoughts and/or prayer for the day

April 2
2 Samuel 13-15

2 Samuel 15:13
"And there came a messenger to David, saying, The hearts of the men of Israel are after Absalom."

In this reading today, Amnon rapes his sister Tamar and then Absolum, their brother, takes vengeance on Amnon and has him killed. Finally Absolum raises up a rebellion against his father, David. When we realize in David's great sin, he had taken advantage of Bathsheba, his spiritual sister, then David has Uriah killed, a spiritual brother, all in rebellion to God his Father, we see very clearly the truth of God's word that says, whatsoever a man sows that he shall reap. This is certainly a reminder to us that we should sow that which will produce the harvest of righteousness instead of seeds of sin and death.

Add your thoughts and/or prayer for the day

April 3
2 Samuel 16-18

2 Samuel 18:33
"And the king was much moved, and went up to the chamber over the gate, and wept: and as he went, thus he said, O my son Absalom, my son, my son Absalom! would God I had died for thee, O Absalom, my son, my son!"

This is a sad ending to a story of rebellion, by a father and then his son. God, our Father, must grieve for those He loves that choose to rebel and neglect His kindness and His guidance. The only difference is that God could and has died for us, his rebellious children, so we might have part in His wonderful kingdom. King David could not offer this kindness because he was rebellious as well, but our King can because He is holy, righteous and full of grace!

Add your thoughts and/or prayer for the day

April 4
2 Samuel 19-21

2 Samuel 19:7
"Now therefore arise, go forth, and speak comfortably unto thy servants: for I swear by the LORD, if thou go not forth, there will not tarry one with thee this night: and that will be worse unto thee than all the evil that befell thee from thy youth until now."

David, having heard the news of Absolum's death, is driven by his emotions to mourn for his son. His faithful friend, Joab, has the intestinal fortitude to confront him and remind him of all those who had fought for him against this enemy are now being confused as to how to respond. They needed a leader that could reassure them, but David's emotions had led him into seclusion. David was right to mourn the loss of his son and Joab was right to call David to leadership. We must be careful about letting our emotions drive our decisions. We must remain faithful to our responsibilities, despite emotions.

Add your thoughts and/or prayer for the day

April 5
2 Samuel 22-24

2 Samuel 22:7-11
"(7) In my distress I called upon the LORD, and cried to my God: and he did hear my voice out of his temple, and my cry did enter into his ears. (8) Then the earth shook and trembled; the foundations of heaven moved and shook, because he was wroth. (9) There went up a smoke out of his nostrils, and fire out of his mouth devoured: coals were kindled by it. (10) He bowed the heavens also, and came down; and darkness was under his feet. (11) And he rode upon a cherub, and did fly: and he was seen upon the wings of the wind."

God answers prayer! When you pray, consider what God does to answer your prayer. For David, the earth shook, the mountains moved, all Heaven bowed as the Lord came to his aid. The Lord wants to do the same for you. Just pray.

Add your thoughts and/or prayer for the day

April 6
1 Kings 1-3

1 Kings 3:6
"And Solomon said, Thou hast shewed unto thy servant David my father great mercy, according as he walked before thee in truth, and in righteousness, and in uprightness of heart with thee; and thou hast kept for him this great kindness, that thou hast given him a son to sit on his throne, as it is this day."

King David had died. Solomon was now king when the Lord appears to him to ask 'what shall I give thee?' In Solomon's response, he exposes a great insight about the impact his father has had on him. Our children see us as we walk before the Lord and it does make a very profound difference if they see us faithful or not. Just remember that your life is the tool God will use to prepare your child for life, marriage, and service to the Lord. Make your life really count for something; let your children see Christ in you by your daily commitment for Him!

Add your thoughts and/or prayer for the day

April 7
1 Kings 4-6

1 Kings 4:29, 34
"(29) And God gave Solomon wisdom and understanding exceeding much, and largeness of heart, even as the sand that is on the sea shore. (34) And there came of all people to hear the wisdom of Solomon, from all kings of the earth, which had heard of his wisdom."

God had given Solomon what he had asked for, wisdom, and he used it for his service to the Lord. God in His grace gives each of us the many gifts of personality, character, and intellect with the goal that we will be able to use these things in His service. Too many use these gifts to their own benefit without ever considering how God could use them in His service. As a result, the work of God suffers. Identify and use the gifts God has given you for His service and don't delay. Start today!

Add your thoughts and/or prayer for the day

April 8
1 Kings 7-9

1 Kings 8:10-11
"(10) And it came to pass, when the priests were come out of the holy place, that the cloud filled the house of the LORD, (11) So that the priests could not stand to minister because of the cloud: for the glory of the LORD had filled the house of the LORD."

Oh how we need the glory of the Lord to fill the house of the Lord in such a way as to drive us out. Man has taken over the house of the Lord; we have polluted its glory with our own. We have been so busy making it what we think it ought to be, instead of letting God just fill it with His glory. In truth, if we were to see God's glory fill the church today, we would not recognize it for what it is, because it is so different than that which we have made it. Please consider what you call worship and ask if this is produced by God or by men? Let's strive to let God's glory fill the church again.

Add your thoughts and/or prayer for the day

April 9
1 Kings 10-12

1 Kings 11:9-10
"(9) And the LORD was angry with Solomon, because his heart was turned from the LORD God of Israel, which had appeared unto him twice, And had commanded him concerning this thing, that he should not go after other gods: but he kept not that which the LORD commanded."

Solomon had been so blessed, spiritually as well as materially by God. only to turn away from the Lord. Why is it, that when God blesses someone with so much that they will turn their back on the Lord and follow other gods? As long as we feel weak, lonely, or impoverished, we seek the Lord in humility, but when He blesses us with the things we need and we begin to feel relief, we take it upon ourselves to walk in our own strength, forgetting God. Remember where your blessings come from, walk in humility and walk in the Spirit!

Add your thoughts and/or prayer for the day

April 10
1 Kings 13-15

1 Kings 15:11
"And Asa did what was right in the eyes of the LORD, as David his father had done."

Asa is the great grandson of David. His grandfather and father had reigned before him over Judah and both of them had led Judah away from the Lord. But now Asa takes a stand for right when the whole country had turned their backs on God, but in doing so he is honored of the Lord. The Lord only needs one person willing to stand for right in order to turn a whole country around. No matter how far away your family or our country has turned from God, you may be that one person God will use to bring them back. But you must be willing to stand alone, if need be. Will you be an Asa or will you be like the rest who just go the way of the crowd?

Add your thoughts and/or prayer for the day

April 11
1 Kings 16-19

1 Kings 19:13
"And it was so, when Elijah heard it, that he wrapped his face in his mantle, and went out, and stood in the entering in of the cave. And, behold, there came a voice unto him, and said, What doest thou here, Elijah?"

Elijah had seen God work in supernatural ways even to the point of praying down fire from Heaven but he had forgotten that God loves to work personally in a still small voice. Our Lord has the ability to do the miraculous and supernatural, but His greatest desire is to seek us out individually in a personal and intimate relationship. God knew what He was going to do and how He was going to do it, but Elijah had lost his direction and purpose. In that moment God, trying to get Elijah engaged again to the Lord's purpose, asks "What are you doing here?" Have you become so wrapped up in the big plan that you have forgotten God seeks an intimate relationship with you? If He were to ask you, "What are you doing here?", would your answer be that which connects you to Him and His desires? A good question for us to consider for today!

Add your thoughts and/or prayer for the day

April 12
1 Kings 20-22

1 Kings 22:8
"And the king of Israel said unto Jehoshaphat, There is yet one man, Micaiah the son of Imlah, by whom we may enquire of the LORD: but I hate him; for he doth not prophesy good concerning me, but evil. And Jehoshaphat said, Let not the king say so."

The king of Israel had surrounded himself with so-called prophets that would tell him what he wanted to hear. Micaiah was a true prophet of God, but Ahab hated him because he would tell him the truth of God's word. We find many today who search out so-called men of God who will tell them what they want to hear to make them feel good. But when a real man of God preaches the truth of God's word, they will turn their backs on the truth. Hopefully you are seeking out that man of God who steadfastly teaches you the word of God without compromise. If so, stand with him, pray for him and appreciate the fact that he is not afraid to tell you the truth.

Add your thoughts and/or prayer for the day

April 13
2 Kings 1-3

2 Kings 2:13-14
"(1) He took up also the mantle of Elijah that fell from him, and went back, and stood by the bank of Jordan; (14) And he took the mantle of Elijah that fell from him, and smote the waters, and said, Where is the LORD God of Elijah? and when he also had smitten the waters, they parted hither and thither: and Elisha went over."

Elisha wanted a double portion of the Lord's power that Elijah had been given, and when it came time God did just that. Elisha realized that it wasn't the man that had the power, but God that gave the man the power. Scripture shows that Elisha did twice as many miracles as did Elijah. We definitely need to hear and realize the power of the Lord God of Elijah, because it is the same God who created the universe, walked with Moses, guided David, protected Israel, came as a baby in Bethlehem, died for us and now lives to save us. Do you recognize that you have living in you the Lord God of Elijah? Then it is time to live like it!

Add your thoughts and/or prayer for the day

April 14
2 Kings 4-6

2 Kings 5:11
"But Naaman was wroth, and went away, and said, Behold, I thought, He will surely come out to me, and stand, and call on the name of the LORD his God, and strike his hand over the place, and recover the leper."

Naaman, a general in the army, had leprosy. The disease was growing in his body, but when told by Elisha that he was to go dip in the dirty Jordan seven times, he almost let his pride keep him from the healing that God was ready to give him. God always honors humility. Pride is so sinful because it is driven by our self-righteousness. God is always ready to bring spiritual healing to those who are willing to empty themselves of pride and humbly submit to the Lord's design for blessing. We must continually guard against pride and walk humbly before the Lord. Has pride gotten in the way of God's blessing for you today?

Add your thoughts and/or prayer for the day

2 Kings 8:18
"And he walked in the way of the kings of Israel, as did the house of Ahab: for the daughter of Ahab was his wife: and he did evil in the sight of the LORD."

This speaks of Joram, the son of the great and godly king of Judah, Jehoshaphat. Joram married the daughter of Ahab and Jezebel and through her influence, his heart was turned against the way of his father and was led by his emotions to do evil in the sight of the Lord. Love is great as an emotion to compel us to care for others, but on the other hand love can make us blind to the realities of poor decisions. Love relationships must be built upon the truth of God's word and in the integrity of both parties to stay committed to their love for God first and foremost. Make sure your love is God's love in the relationship and not some carnal lustful love that separates you from God's influence.

Add your thoughts and/or prayer for the day

April 16
2 Kings 10-13

2 Kings 12:2
"And Jehoash did that which was right in the sight of the LORD all his days wherein Jehoiada the priest instructed him."

In our reading, trying to follow the kings of Israel and Judah can be difficult, but we notice that the good kings seem to be in Judah. Here we read of Jehoash and find that his good standing with God was propagated by his association with Jehoiada, the priest. Kind of tells you what kind of man this priest was. Truth is that we need each other to encourage us in our walk with the Lord. The Bible tells us that there is safety in the multitude of counselors. Who is your spiritual encourager? Better yet, who is it that you might encourage today? You never know, but that word of encouragement could save a life, a family, or a country.

Add your thoughts and/or prayer for the day

April 17
2 Kings 14-16

2 Kings 16:3
"But he walked in the way of the kings of Israel, yea, and made his son to pass through the fire, according to the abominations of the heathen, whom the LORD cast out from before the children of Israel."

The phrase, *"made his son to pass through the fire"* indicates that in their worship of other gods, parents would sacrifice their children by burning them on an altar. Unimaginable, right? Yet, there are those who claim they are Christ's that are sacrificing their children on altars every day; the altar of 'too busy' or 'making it better for my kids'. Our children need some moms and dads who will teach them the importance of serving the one true God, reading the scriptures together, attending church together, praying together. Don't be guilty of sacrificing your children on an altar to other gods.

Add your thoughts and/or prayer for the day

April 18
2 Kings 17-19

2 Kings 18:4
"He removed the high places, and brake the images, and cut down the groves, and brake in pieces the brazen serpent that Moses had made: for unto those days the children of Israel did burn incense to it: and he called it Nehushtan."

Hezekiah was a good king. He wanted to serve only the Lord, so he destroyed all the things the people had come to use in their worship that did not honor the Lord. God had given the children of Israel healing from a plague by Moses making this brass serpent that they were to look upon for healing. They had taken it and now made it an object of worship instead of God. Many Christians do the same with things like crosses, statues of saints, and church buildings. Be sure you're worshipping the Lord and not the religious stuff. He deserves our worship, all of it!

Add your thoughts and/or prayer for the day

April 19
2 Kings 20-22

2 Kings 22:13
"Go ye, enquire of the LORD for me, and for the people, and for all Judah, concerning the words of this book that is found: for great is the wrath of the LORD that is kindled against us, because our fathers have not hearkened unto the words of this book, to do according unto all that which is written concerning us."

During the course of several kings who would not follow the Lord, the Law had been lost in the rubble of the temple, but now it is found and a young king, Josiah, is desirous to follow the Lord. It doesn't take many generations to get a family completely removed from following Christ, but it only takes one to stand up for right and bring a whole nation back to the Lord. Let's pray that our leaders might find the word of God that has been put out of the government and come back to serving the Lord from its truths.

Add your thoughts and/or prayer for the day

April 20
2 Kings 23-25

2 Kings 25:13
"And the pillars of brass that were in the house of the LORD, and the bases, and the brasen sea that was in the house of the LORD, did the Chaldees break in pieces, and carried the brass of them to Babylon."

How sad to read of the capture of Judah, the destruction of Jerusalem and Solomon's temple; this mighty city, the wonderful feasts and joy around the worship of God at the Temple, now being turned to rubble. Why had this happened; all because the people of God refused to allow God to be the rightful king and ruler of their lives. Guard your hearts, which are now the temple of God! Refusing to let the Lord rule and reign there will cost you the joy and victory He brings only to be captured by the world that will enslave you to emptiness, discouragement and defeat.

Add your thoughts and/or prayer for the day

April 21
1 Chronicles 1-4

1 Chronicles 4:10
"And Jabez called on the God of Israel, saying, Oh that thou wouldest bless me indeed, and enlarge my coast, and that thine hand might be with me, and that thou wouldest keep me from evil, that it may not grieve me! And God granted him that which he requested."

In this large amount of scripture of genealogies and appointments there is this small verse about a man named Jabez. A great deal was made about this sometime back and people were in a flurry about 'praying the prayer of Jabez' as if it had some special power with God. Truth is that Jabez prays and the Lord answers his prayer. Our Lord is concerned about our prayers. He listens, and He answers. He has the right to answer as He wills, either 'yes', 'no', or 'not at this time', but He always answers our prayers and He will answer them in a way that benefits us for our best. Just pray and accept by faith His answer!

Add your thoughts and/or prayer for the day

1 Chronicles 6:31-32 ESV
"(31) These are the men whom David put in charge of the service of song in the house of the LORD after the ark rested there. (32) They ministered with song before the tabernacle of the tent of meeting until Solomon built the house of the LORD in Jerusalem, and they performed their service according to their order."

David understood the importance of music when it came to the worship of God. These men were the singers and musicians and what is most interesting is that they performed their service according to their order, meaning that they did their ministry faithfully. It is important for anyone gifted in ministry to always be available and willing to use that gift for the Lord. It is not given to an individual to be an entertainer or performer, but to be a minister. Every song should be viewed as a sermon set to music. If God has gifted you with music, then use it faithfully and humbly out of a heart of service and love for the Savior, not as an act of performance or self glory.

Add your thoughts and/or prayer for the day

April 23
1 Chronicles 8-10

1 Chronicles 10:13
"So Saul died for his breach of faith. He broke faith with the LORD in that he did not keep the command of the LORD, and also consulted a medium, seeking guidance."

The story of the life of Saul is a sad one. It is the story of a life that could have been. If only he had maintained his faith and obedience to God, he could have been a great king of Israel, but because he decided to do things his own way, against the will of God, he lost everything. How many times have we exchanged what could have been God's best for us for a cheap substitute that left us empty and defeated, because we thought we knew what was best for us. We should take the lesson of Saul's life to heart. The last thing we should want is to end our lives with the thought of what it could have been, if only we had obeyed the Lord. Receive the best of God by following Him by faith!

Add your thoughts and/or prayer for the day

1 Chronicles 12:38
"All these, men of war, arrayed in battle order, came to Hebron with full intent to make David king over all Israel. Likewise, all the rest of Israel were of a single mind to make David king."

Men came from every tribe of Israel to show their support for David, the new king. Reading these names and seeing the mass numbers of men who came to David's support, just reminded me of the need for godly men to stand together supporting and encouraging each other in the work of God. God has raised up a mighty army in the church to support and encourage each other, but in these days, it seems that many of our ranks have left their posts and are finding other things to occupy their time. The army of God now is made up of only a few of the many it should have available for service. If you have neglected your post, please consider the discouragement it is causing to those who need your support.

Add your thoughts and/or prayer for the day

April 25
1 Chronicles 14-16

1 Chronicles 16:23-25
"(23) Sing unto the LORD, all the earth; shew forth from day to day his salvation. (24) Declare his glory among the heathen; his marvellous works among all nations. (25) For great is the LORD, and greatly to be praised: he also is to be feared above all gods."

This is just a part of the song that David had sung at the return of the Ark of the Covenant to Jerusalem. It was truly a song of praise and you can just imagine how awesome it must have sounded as all the people sang it together. God never gets tired of our praise. He hears it and it comes to Him as a sweet aroma before Him. The more we praise Him, the more our hearts are reminded of how good He is to us. Go ahead lift up your voice and sing praise to the one who deserves our praise and honor. The Lord, He is worthy of ALL praise!

Add your thoughts and/or prayer for the day

April 26
1 Chronicles 17-19

1 Chronicles 17:20
"O LORD, there is none like thee, neither is there any God beside thee, according to all that we have heard with our ears."

David, overwhelmed at God's goodness acknowledges the Lord's greatness in this prayer of praise. Haven't you ever been alone at some point and begin to consider all that God has done for you and just have to blurt out a praise to Him? The enemy loves to get us concentrating on all that we think we don't have, because by doing that we get discouraged and despondent. But if you will stop and consider all that you have that you can praise the Lord for, it will begin to overwhelm you and like David you will have to say, *"O Lord, there is none like you".* What one thing can you praise the Lord for right now? Then consider the next and the next and before long you won't be able to stop praising Him.

Add your thoughts and/or prayer for the day

1 Chronicles 21:29-30
"(29) For the tabernacle of the LORD, which Moses made in the wilderness, and the altar of the burnt offering, were at that season in the high place at Gibeon. (30) But David could not go before it to enquire of God: for he was afraid because of the sword of the angel of the LORD."

David, filled with pride, had required his general to number the people of his kingdom. Now convicted of his wrong, he feels that he cannot speak to the Lord as he had before, because of fear. The Lord hates a prideful heart. Pride tells us that we are something when the Word of God tells us we can do nothing without Christ. Any sin separates us from true fellowship with our Father. The best thing we can do is guard our hearts from sin and when we fail, take care to confess it immediately! Don't miss a minute of fellowship with your Father.

Add your thoughts and/or prayer for the day

1 Chronicles 24:19
"These were the orderings of them in their service to come into the house of the LORD, according to their manner, under Aaron their father, as the LORD God of Israel had commanded him."

The great king David was a meticulous leader, even in the setting in order the house of the Lord. Each man twenty years old and up had a job, a place of service. Each one was to take his responsibility very seriously, understanding that the Lord had established the work they were to do. Today the Lord's work suffers as a second-hand, bottom-of-the-list, and as an 'if-I-have-time' event. Oh, that today's church had more such committed workers. Men and women who saw that whatever the task in the church was, it was an important one that needed to be seriously considered and accomplished for the simple reason that it is the Lord's work. The Lord deserves our best!

Add your thoughts and/or prayer for the day

April 29
1 Chronicles 27-29

1 Chronicles 29:11-12
"(11) *Thine, O LORD, is the greatness, and the power, and the glory, and the victory, and the majesty: for all that is in the heaven and in the earth is thine; thine is the kingdom, O LORD, and thou art exalted as head above all. (12) Both riches and honour come of thee, and thou reignest over all; and in thine hand is power and might; and in thine hand it is to make great, and to give strength unto all.*"

If you think of yourself as a "self-made" man or woman, guess again! No matter whom we think we are or how much we think we have gained or done for ourselves, nothing was done without God's involvement. Remain humble before the Lord; acknowledge all that He has done for you and always praise Him for all that you have. Be always ready to give out of the abundance He has given you.

Add your thoughts and/or prayer for the day

April 30
2 Chronicles 1-3

2 Chronicles 2:5-6
"(5) And the house which I build is great: for great is our God above all gods. (6) But who is able to build him an house, seeing the heaven and heaven of heavens cannot contain him? who am I then, that I should build him an house, save only to burn sacrifice before him?"

When considering building the first temple, Solomon is overwhelmed with the idea of it. How can anyone think that our God could be contained in a building? Yet, most of us keep God nicely tucked away in some kind of box we have designed that only allows him access to part of our life. We think we can conveniently pull Him out when we need Him and ignore Him the rest of the time. Truth is that God will not be confined to just your box. He is God and Lord over all. Do not try to hem Him in, but instead acknowledge His Lordship over all you are and all you have, then you will be living the abundant life He has promised you.

Add your thoughts and/or prayer for the day

May 1
2 Chronicles 4-6

2 Chronicles 5:13-14
"(13) ...when they lifted up their voice with the trumpets and cymbals and instruments of musick, and praised the LORD, saying, For he is good; for his mercy endureth for ever: that then the house was filled with a cloud, even the house of the LORD; (14) So that the priests could not stand to minister by reason of the cloud: for the glory of the LORD had filled the house of God."

The temple had been built and with the Ark of the Covenant in place, now was the time for music and praise! When the people's hearts are turned toward God and their songs and praise is strictly from the heart, God's presence will always be felt. If you participate in music ministry, please note the importance God places on your calling. Do not seek the popularity or self glory of a performance, but that God's glory fills the place. Be faithful, be whole-hearted, and be true to your calling!

Add your thoughts and/or prayer for the day

May 2
2 Chronicles 7-9

2 Chronicles 7:3
"And when all the children of Israel saw how the fire came down, and the glory of the LORD upon the house, they bowed themselves with their faces to the ground upon the pavement, and worshipped, and praised the LORD, saying, For he is good; for his mercy endureth for ever."

What an awesome event to have been able to witness as the Lord's presence was seen and felt by the people of God. How in that moment they were unable to do anything but bow and worship the Lord. Oh, that the Lord's presence would be so real again in the house of God. We now are the temple of God and we should seek daily to have this kind of encounter with the Lord so that His presence in our lives might be so real that we could not stand but would bow before Him declaring His goodness to us.

Add your thoughts and/or prayer for the day

May 3
2 Chronicles 10-12

2 Chronicles 12:1
"And it came to pass, when Rehoboam had established the kingdom, and had strengthened himself, he forsook the law of the LORD, and all Israel with him."

Rehoboam, as leader of Judah makes a decision to turn his back on the law of the Lord. Notice that all Israel follows. God is the one that establishes authority and in so doing, it is His desire that we follow Him. When we choose to go our own way, we must remember that others will be influenced. In our homes today, God has established the authority of the husband and wife as parents. Yet, how many times have we acted in our own selfish design and violated God's leadership to follow after our own interests never thinking about how many lives are being influenced by our decision. We really need to be careful; someone is always watching and following our lead.

Add your thoughts and/or prayer for the day

2 Chronicles 15:3-4
"(3) For a long time Israel was without the true God, and without a teaching priest and without law, (4) but when in their distress they turned to the LORD, the God of Israel, and sought him, he was found by them."

Reading the history of Israel, it is like a roller coaster of ups and downs. In one place, they are wholly committed to the Lord and experiencing His many blessings. In another, they have turned their backs on Him and are in all kinds of trouble. It would be easy to speak of their failures, except for the fact that we live in much the same way. Just as they lived without the Lord, without a 'teaching priest' and without God's word is common to anyone who is living for themselves. When we want to be in charge of our lives, we don't want the Lord, a preacher or the Bible to get in the way of what we want, but it always leads to times of distress. How good God is, because even in our willful acts to exclude Him, when in trouble He is always there to be found when we seek Him.

Add your thoughts and/or prayer for the day

May 5
2 Chronicles 16-18

2 Chronicles 16:9
"For the eyes of the LORD run to and fro throughout the whole earth, to shew himself strong in the behalf of them whose heart is perfect toward him. Herein thou hast done foolishly: therefore from henceforth thou shalt have wars."

Asa, king of Judah, had hired another country to save him from the attacks of Basha, king of Israel, instead of trusting God to protect him and as a result lost an opportunity God had prepared for him. Just as then, God is still looking for those who will wholly trust in the Lord and allow Him to be in control of those situations that seem so threatening. In everything, the Lord has a plan for our good, but how many times do those plans get sabotaged by our desire to be in control? Remember that we are only victors when God is in control!

Add your thoughts and/or prayer for the day

May 6
2 Chronicles 19-21

2 Chronicles 20:17
"You will not need to fight in this battle. Stand firm, hold your position, and see the salvation of the LORD on your behalf, O Judah and Jerusalem.' Do not be afraid and do not be dismayed. Tomorrow go out against them, and the LORD will be with you."

Jehoshaphat was facing an army that he could not defeat and he called for the whole country to pray. The word of God came through a prophet telling them that the battle was not theirs but the Lords. If only when we are faced with those insurmountable situations, we would learn to *"stand firm and see the salvation of the Lord"*. We get anxious as we see it approaching and we start to get busy in our strength to try and take charge, but if we would just learn to stand still and put our trust in the Lord, then we would see His victory in the situation, and He would get the glory.

Add your thoughts and/or prayer for the day

2 Chronicles 24:18-19
"(18) And they left the house of the LORD God of their fathers, and served groves and idols: and wrath came upon Judah and Jerusalem for this their trespass. (19) Yet he sent prophets to them, to bring them again unto the LORD; and they testified against them: but they would not give ear."

After years of putting God first, the people left off serving the Lord, but the Lord would not give up and kept sending men of God to call them back, even though they would not listen. There are those who were raised up in the church, being taught and led to serve the Lord, but who have left the church to serve themselves in the ways of the world. God will not give up on them and neither should we. No matter how far they drift away, at every opportunity we should love and encourage them in the Lord. We are called to the restoration business.

Add your thoughts and/or prayer for the day

2 Chronicles 25:15
"Therefore the LORD was angry with Amaziah and sent to him a prophet, who said to him, "Why have you sought the gods of a people who did not deliver their own people from your hand?"

The king had won a great victory against his enemy by listening and obeying the Lord's commands. Yet, when he returned home, he took the false gods of the enemy he had just defeated and set them up to be his gods. How foolish! Yet, in the same way we will see God giving us victory in our lives over the enemy that comes to kill, steal and destroy and then in the next breath serve the enemy again by yielding to his temptations. Why do we so easily follow after one whose only desire is to destroy us, when we could be following the one whose only desire is to love us?

Add your thoughts and/or prayer for the day

2 Chronicles 28-30

2 Chronicles 29:28-29
"(28) And all the congregation worshipped, and the singers sang, and the trumpeters sounded: and all this continued until the burnt offering was finished. (29) And when they had made an end of offering, the king and all that were present with him bowed themselves, and worshipped."

The king had ordered the House of God to be cleansed and to restore the worship that had been halted by the previous king. As they performed the sacrifices and sang praises, it so moved the king and those nearby, that when it was completed, they continued to humbly worship the Lord. It just reminds us that true worship extends beyond the boundaries of form or ritual. It flows out of a heart that is overwhelmed by the awesome grace of our Lord. Have you been overwhelmed lately?

Add your thoughts and/or prayer for the day

May 10
2 Chronicles 31-33

2 Chronicles 32:7-8
"(7) Be strong and courageous, be not afraid nor dismayed for the king of Assyria, nor for all the multitude that is with him: for there be more with us than with him: (8) With him is an arm of flesh; but with us is the LORD our God to help us, and to fight our battles. And the people rested themselves upon the words of Hezekiah king of Judah."

Hezekiah had led the country back to the Lord and now a worldly king comes, thinking that in Judah's choosing to serve only one god would make them weak. Little did he realize as Hezekiah did, that with God they had become the majority? When we choose to make God the Lord of our lives, we have been given the ability to stand in the onslaught of the enemy's attacks with confidence that in Christ, we are more than conquerors. Be strong and courageous. dear child of God, you have all you need in Him!

Add your thoughts and/or prayer for the day

Chronicles 34:3
"For in the eighth year of (Josiah's) reign, while he was yet young, he began to seek after the God of David his father: and in the twelfth year he began to purge Judah and Jerusalem from the high places, and the groves, and the carved images, and the molten images."

The story of Josiah is an awesome example of how a young man, dedicated to the Lord can make a big difference in the world in which he lives. Josiah was 16 when he began to seek the Lord instead of following the example of his father, Amon, who was a wicked king; Josiah chose to follow the example of godly men. Every young man should consider the decisions he is making and follow the example of Josiah to seek the Lord and break down any strongholds that the enemy has been allowed to establish in their lives to serve the one true God. Follow the example of godly men and make a difference in this world that so desperately needs godly leadership.

Add your thoughts and/or prayer for the day

May 12
Ezra 1-4

Ezra 1:1-2
"(1) Now in the first year of Cyrus king of Persia, that the word of the LORD by the mouth of Jeremiah might be fulfilled, the LORD stirred up the spirit of Cyrus king of Persia, that he made a proclamation throughout all his kingdom, and put it also in writing, saying, (2) Thus saith Cyrus king of Persia, The LORD God of heaven hath given me all the kingdoms of the earth; and he hath charged me to build him an house at Jerusalem, which is in Judah."

Cyrus was a heathen king of Persia, ruling over the Israelites at this time. Amazingly, Cyrus realizes that as powerful as he was in the world, he acknowledges that God had given him everything. We need to pray for our leaders, that they would remember they answer to a higher authority than public opinion. Pray for God to stir them up like He did this king.

Add your thoughts and/or prayer for the day

May 13
Ezra 5-7

Ezra 7:6
"This Ezra went up from Babylon; and he was a ready scribe in the law of Moses, which the LORD God of Israel had given: and the king granted him all his request, according to the hand of the LORD his God upon him."

Ezra was a priest, not a statesman or a builder. Yet God gave this man such favor with the heathen kings who ruled over Israel at this time, that he was allowed to take whoever he wanted to rebuild the temple in Jerusalem and to do it with the complete funding of these kings' treasuries. God is not short of turning the hearts of heathen kings to act in his favor, but it came as a result of one man who was totally yielded to seeking the law of the Lord and doing it. Ezra's commitment to the Lord produced an open link for the Lord to act upon the hearts of these kings. When we guard our hearts to do what is right in the sight of God, it is then that the Lord can access those around us more readily to accomplish His will in their lives as well.

Add your thoughts and/or prayer for the day

May 14
Ezra 8-10

Ezra 9:5-6
"(5) And at the evening sacrifice I rose from my fasting, with my garment and my cloak torn, and fell upon my knees and spread out my hands to the LORD my God, (6) saying: "O my God, I am ashamed and blush to lift my face to you, my God, for our iniquities have risen higher than our heads, and our guilt has mounted up to the heavens."

Ezra, the spiritual leader, was overwhelmed at the people whom God had so graciously delivered from bondage, only to enter right back into sin. In much the same way, as Christians, we have been given the greatest gift of all in receiving God's gift of grace unto salvation, yet we struggle with sin. We find ourselves, instead of living in this awesome liberty of grace, to be continually struggling with guilt under the bondage of sin. There is something far better for us than living in this guilt and discouragement, we should repent, confess our sins and receive the forgiveness the Lord offers us, and then walk responsibly in the liberty of grace. Now that is how the Lord would have us live!

Add your thoughts and/or prayer for the day

May 15
Nehemiah 1-3

Nehemiah 3:5
"And next to them the Tekoites repaired, but their nobles would not stoop to serve their Lord."

In any work, you will find those who are the 'party poopers', they just don't want to get their hands dirty. For the people of Jerusalem, everyone was involved in rebuilding the city wall. Each group had a section to complete. I am sure that the Tekoites were disappointed at their nobles' response, but even though it meant they had to do more, they did not let it stop them from serving the Lord by doing the work that was required. Too many times we have seen where the lack of involvement of others has been the excuse for not doing the work at all. Don't let others non-involvement discourage you from the blessing of being used by God. Whether anyone joins you or not, just serve the Lord!

Add your thoughts and/or prayer for the day

May 16
Nehemiah 4-6

Nehemiah 6:15-16
"(15) So the wall was finished in the twenty and fifth day of the month Elul, in fifty and two days. (16) And it came to pass, that when all our enemies heard thereof, and all the heathen that were about us saw these things, they were much cast down in their own eyes: for they perceived that this work was wrought of our God."

The great Jerusalem had lain in ruins until Nehemiah showed up to rebuild the wall. The task had been so great that no one had thought it could be done, but under the Lord's direction, what seemed impossible was done in short order. God's plan, led by God's man, with the cooperation of God's people, equals great success. Instead of being discouraged, or frightened by the enemy, this people had a mind to work and as a result, the world saw what God could do. God can do it again, but we must be willing to work together and complete the tasks God gives us. Just don't quit!

Add your thoughts and/or prayer for the day

Nehemiah 8:8-9
"(8) So they read in the book in the law of God distinctly, and gave the sense, and caused them to understand the reading. (9) And Nehemiah, which is the Tirshatha, and Ezra the priest the scribe, and the Levites that taught the people, said unto all the people, This day is holy unto the LORD your God; mourn not, nor weep. For all the people wept, when they heard the words of the law."

What a broken people! After rebuilding the wall and finally coming back to the place of their ancestors, they gather to have the word of God read to them and at its very reading, they weep. How the Lord must yearn for the church to have this kind of attitude and desire to hear and respond to His word today. Pray for the church's brokenness to return, that true revival might begin and the cold indifferent heart might be humbled and tender to voice of God. Pray that it begin with us!

Add your thoughts and/or prayer for the day

May 18
Nehemiah 10-13

Nehemiah 13:11
"Then contended I with the rulers, and said, Why is the house of God forsaken? And I gathered them together, and set them in their place."

The house of God and the commitment to worship had declined in Jerusalem shortly after the city-wide jubilation of the completion of the wall. Much like we did after the 9/11 attacks when people flooded into the church, then within weeks the numbers had dwindled back to the norm. We live in a time when the times of God are no longer honored and the house of God is neglected. God gets our hand-me-downs and our leftovers. It is time that God got the best we can give and the first of our time, talent and treasure. Please examine yourself in these areas, God deserves your best, your first and your all.

Add your thoughts and/or prayer for the day

May 19
Esther 1-4

Esther 4:14
"For if thou altogether holdest thy peace at this time, then shall there enlargement and deliverance arise to the Jews from another place; but thou and thy father's house shall be destroyed: and who knoweth whether thou art come to the kingdom for such a time as this?"

Mordecai, facing death, encourages Esther to speak up for the Jews. His faith is heard when he tells her that if she fails to do this, God would send help from another. Nothing can happen without God's knowledge, so when faced with difficult circumstances, our faith carries us in to the reality that we are not in these times alone nor by chance; God is in control. Instead of fear, let your faith guide you into a sense of security, knowing you are with the Shepherd who will never leave you nor forsake you, but will go with you and give you the strength you need *"for such a time as this."*

Add your thoughts and/or prayer for the day

May 20
Esther 5-7

Esther 6:13
"And Haman told Zeresh his wife and all his friends every thing that had befallen him. Then said his wise men and Zeresh his wife unto him, If Mordecai be of the seed of the Jews, before whom thou hast begun to fall, thou shalt not prevail against him, but shalt surely fall before him."

It is interesting that Haman's wife and counselors acknowledge that a slave of Jewish descent would have such power as to overtake this government leader. Although it does not say it, they had come to understand the power of God which protected the Jewish people. Many times, people in positions of power will try and demonstrate their authority by challenging God's institutions, but when God begins to move to protect His own, you can be sure the opposition has no leg to stand on. It's always good to be on God's side!

Add your thoughts and/or prayer for the day

Esther 9:4
"For Mordecai was great in the king's house, and his fame went out throughout all the provinces: for this man Mordecai waxed greater and greater."

This is the result of a man who stood for God, despite the possible persecution by Haman, a high-ranking government official. How awesome it is to see God honor someone who would not bow to those who opposed his God. When you read the accounts of the people of faith in Hebrews 11, you find that there were those who received honor while here on earth, but there were others whose honor was bestowed on them after dying for a cause. When we make a stand for the Lord, it may not always turn out with the kind of acceptance as it did for Mordecai, but it is always right to stand for what is right.

Add your thoughts and/or prayer for the day

May 22
Job 1-3

Job 1:20-21
"(20) Then Job arose, and rent his mantle, and shaved his head, and fell down upon the ground, and worshipped, (21) And said, Naked came I out of my mother's womb, and naked shall I return thither: the LORD gave, and the LORD hath taken away; blessed be the name of the LORD."

In the midst of the worst of circumstances and extreme loss, Job worships the Lord. For most people when tragedies hit, they seem to want to blame God. Not Job, he worships God. It is true, that either your circumstances will control you or you will control the circumstances. However, being believers, we understand that it is best when God is in control. Even if we don't understand the purpose for them, God does have a plan. So go ahead and worship the Lord through those times of uncertainty because He is the one who holds you in the palm of His hands.

Add your thoughts and/or prayer for the day

Job 7:17-18
"(17) What is man, that thou shouldest magnify him? and that thou shouldest set thine heart upon him? (18) And that thou shouldest visit him every morning, and try him every moment?"

Job, in the midst of all his trouble, reminds himself of the truth that God is always faithful. As we all know, circumstances of life can and do become overwhelming. When that happens, it is a natural course of man to turn inward; making everything about one's self, without considering there is a much bigger plan in progress. If in your life you are facing those times without answers, just stop and consider all that God does for us. Consider that the Creator of the universe has deemed you worthy to love and that He is always with you to see you through every situation. God will always be faithful!

Add your thoughts and/or prayer for the day

May 24
Job 8-10

Job 8:5-7 ESV
"(5) If you will seek God and plead with the Almighty for mercy, (6) if you are pure and upright, surely then he will rouse himself for you and restore your rightful habitation. (7) And though your beginning was small, your latter days will be very great."

Here Job's friend thought he knew why Job was suffering and is pleading with Job to confess his sins and get right; then God would bless him with prosperity. <u>Oh how wrong he was!</u> Little did he know that he was speaking to a man that God had singled out because of his righteous integrity. We know that God does chastise his children when they sin and that we need to confess our sin to remain in fellowship with the Father, but before we judge another, we might consider that sometimes God uses conflict to teach lessons to the righteous that we cannot learn in any other way. He also will use our afflictions to bring about His glory through our responses or to meet a need in another's life. Don't be so quick to judge yourself or others for their seeming problems, you might just be wrong.

<u>Add your thoughts and/or prayer for the day</u>

Job 11:7-8
"(7) Canst thou by searching find out God? canst thou find out the Almighty unto perfection? (8) It is as high as heaven; what canst thou do? deeper than hell; what canst thou know?"

The friend of Job, even though wrong about Job's situation, makes a great declaration about God and man's knowledge of Him. There are those who have studied the scriptures all their lives and realize that no matter how much they have studied, God is still a mystery, full of wonder and awe and they humbly admit their lack of understanding. Then you will meet those, who in their arrogance, have God all figured out. They have all the answers and their pride tells you that they have not yet met the God whose presence sends men prostrate to the floor in worship. No matter how much you know, you still do not know all that there is to know of God, but in your seeking, the Lord says He will be found.

Add your thoughts and/or prayer for the day

Job 16:19-21
"(19) *Even now, behold, my witness is in heaven, and he who testifies for me is on high. (20) My friends scorn me; my eye pours out tears to God, (21) that he would argue the case of a man with God, as a son of man does with his neighbor.*"

As Job's friends continue to rag on Job, trying to expose some sin that he must have done in order to receive such woes, he is reminded that he has an advocate in heaven. John tells us that Jesus is the advocate for the redeemed and continually defends us against the Devil's accusations. When in the flesh we fail the Lord, the Lord never fails to defend us in the Spirit where our salvation is established. The enemy has no argument that the Lord can't defend, based upon His redemption price paid at Calvary. We are under the blood!

Add your thoughts and/or prayer for the day

May 27
Job 18-20

Job 19:25-27
"(25) For I know that my Redeemer lives, and at the last he will stand upon the earth. (26) And after my skin has been thus destroyed, yet in my flesh I shall see God, (27) whom I shall see for myself, and my eyes shall behold, and not another. My heart faints within me!"

Facing the torment of loss and physical illness and in his own thoughts possible death, Job finds solace in the thought of his Redeemer! When we are in the conditions of life that tend to force us to consider our mortality, it is a great time to step back and remember there is a much bigger plan --- God's plan! If He is your redeemer, then you too, will find a great peace in knowing that what the world sees as the end, we see as the great beginning. Oh, to see our Redeemer face-to-face for the first time will surely be glorious beyond measure!

Add your thoughts and/or prayer for the day

May 28
Job 21-24

Job 23:8-10
*"(8) Behold, I go forward, but he is not there; and backward,
but I cannot perceive him: (9) On the left hand, where he
doth work, but I cannot behold him: he hideth himself on the
right hand, that I cannot see him: (10) But he knoweth the
way that I take: when he hath tried me,
I shall come forth as gold."*

Job wants to plead his case before the Lord, but in his heart, he knows that God is at work in his life, working to produce good. Even though it sometimes seems that the Lord is not there with you, you can be sure He is! Those are the times He is producing the qualities of your life that He deems to be most valuable. Instead of complaining or accusing God for the problems, look for Him in the crevices of your heart and you will find Him there digging for gold.

Add your thoughts and/or prayer for the day

May 29
Job 25-28

Job 28:28
"And unto man he said, Behold, the fear of the Lord, that is wisdom; and to depart from evil is understanding."

What a great passage for us this morning! Job presents the hunt for wisdom and in doing so, leads us through the wonder and awe of all that God has created; yet the greatest thing God offers man is wisdom and understanding. The conclusion for us then is as Job says, to fear God and depart from evil. Truth is that they go hand in hand. The more we learn of God, the more we reverence and sit in awe of Him. The more we are in awe of God, the more we want to honor Him with our lives by turning from evil. What a mighty God we serve; Angels bow before Him, Heaven and Earth adore Him; what a mighty God we serve!

Add your thoughts and/or prayer for the day

May 30
Job 29-32

Job 31:13-15
"(13) If I did despise the cause of my manservant or of my maidservant, when they contended with me; (14) What then shall I do when God riseth up? and when he visiteth, what shall I answer him? (15) Did not he that made me in the womb make him? and did not one fashion us in the womb?"

We need to be reminded like Job, that we are superior to no one. God is no respecter of persons, meaning that He puts us all on the same plain. Although we are all different, we were all created by the same Creator, and the Lord loves us all. That is why the Lord, in describing the law, said that it is important that as we love God, we must also love one another. Guard your spirit today from thinking you are better than someone else and instead, serve each with love and compassion.

Add your thoughts and/or prayer for the day

May 31
Job 33-35

Job 33:13-14 ESV
"(13) Why do you contend against him, saying, 'He will answer none of man's words'? (14) For God speaks in one way, and in two, though man does not perceive it."

The young Elihu gives some great advice after listening to Job complain that God would not hear him, that in some way God had turned against him. You see, God answers every prayer; to some it is "yes", to some it is "no", and to some it is "not now", but God answers them all. The problem does not lie in God giving an answer; the problem lies in us not accepting God's answer for us. Remember this; if you can in some way manipulate God to do what you want, then you have become God. Our desire should be to be conformed to the image of Jesus, praying, "not my will, but thine be done."

Add your thoughts and/or prayer for the day

June 1
Job 36-38

Job 38:1-4
"(1) Then the LORD answered Job out of the whirlwind and said: (2) "Who is this that darkens counsel by words without knowledge? (3) Dress for action like a man; I will question you, and you make it known to me. (4) "Where were you when I laid the foundation of the earth? Tell me, if you have understanding."

When we come before the Lord with our complaints of how He has determined to care for us, we are like spoiled children who will argue with their parents without understanding the love and sacrifice they have made for us. Learn from Job. When God speaks, there is no argument. Instead of complaining for what you think God has not done, consider all that He has done, then be quiet before Him and be consumed by His awesome love for you.

Add your thoughts and/or prayer for the day

June 2
Job 39-42

Job 42:2-3
"(2) I know that thou canst do every thing, and that no thought can be withholden from thee. (3) Who is he that hideth counsel without knowledge? therefore have I uttered that I understood not; things too wonderful for me, which I knew not."

Reading through the tragedies that Job has encountered and then hearing his friends berate him, painting God out to be a hardened task master, we can sympathize with him in his calamity. We have all been in that place where our circumstances have turned us to a selfish outlook crying, "why me?" Here we are reminded that we don't have to understand everything God does or why, but we should remember that He loves us, that He is able to do what He wants and that He truly is too wonderful for us.

Add your thoughts and/or prayer for the day

June 3
Psalms 1-5

Psalms 4:3-4
*"(3) But know that the LORD hath set apart him that is godly
for himself: the LORD will hear when I call unto him. (4)
Stand in awe, and sin not: commune with your own heart
upon your bed, and be still."*

The reward of the one who seeks godliness is to know that God will use him; that God will hear him. What an awesome thought, that the totally sovereign Creator God sets you apart unto Himself as special! So how are we to be 'godly'? He tells us! Stand in awe of the relationship you have with God, turn from sin when it raises its ugly head, 'commune' or be in close relationship, sharing and listening as you spend time with Him, and then just be still! Isn't God just awesome to want to be in love with us?

Add your thoughts and/or prayer for the day

June 4
Psalms 6-8

Psalms 8:3-5
"(3) When I consider thy heavens, the work of thy fingers, the moon and the stars, which thou hast ordained; (4) What is man, that thou art mindful of him? and the son of man, that thou visitest him? (5) For thou hast made him a little lower than the angels, and hast crowned him with glory and honour."

Sitting under a starry night and considering how vast this universe is, causes my mind to go into overload. But then consider that the one who created all of this cares so deeply for us that He was willing to die for us; that is just overwhelming! Yet, it is true! God loves you with all His heart. He has crowned you with His glory and honored you with life in His presence. How do you bring glory to one who loves you this much?

Add your thoughts and/or prayer for the day

June 5
Psalm 9-12

Psalms 9:1-2
"(1) I will praise thee, O LORD, with my whole heart; I will shew forth all thy marvellous works. (2) I will be glad and rejoice in thee: I will sing praise to thy name, O thou most High."

David says he will praise the Lord with his whole heart. Now that is the way to praise the Lord, not holding anything back, not letting those hidden things prevent us from real open-hearted worship. If we are going to experience this kind of worship, then we must begin by experiencing God's complete forgiveness. To think that God has wiped our slate clean and called us righteous; that is one marvelous work we definitely should be glad and rejoicing over. Go ahead, sing that song of praise! Don't let anything keep you from whole heartedly praising the one who deserves all of our praise.

Add your thoughts and/or prayer for the day

June 6
Psalm 13-17

Psalms 16:8, 11
"(8) I have set the LORD always before me: because he is at my right hand, I shall not be moved. (11) "Thou wilt shew me the path of life: in thy presence is fulness of joy; at thy right hand there are pleasures for evermore."

What a promise David had found in the Lord. Making the decision to always let the Lord have the preeminence in our lives will give us the ability to stand when the storms of life come railing against us. That means He is "before" us and we follow Him! Not the other way around. This promise could be ours. God will guide us, if we will be led. Real joy will be found when we are with Him and the success of life is found at His side. What are we waiting for? If He did that for David, He will do it for us!

Add your thoughts and/or prayer for the day

June 7
Psalm 18-21

Psalms 19:9-11
"(9) The fear of the LORD is clean, enduring for ever: the judgments of the LORD are true and righteous altogether. (10) More to be desired are they than gold, yea, than much fine gold: sweeter also than honey and the honeycomb. (11) Moreover by them is thy servant warned: and in keeping of them there is great reward."

It is easy for us to forget how valuable and sweet are the commands of our Lord as found in the word of God. Nothing on this earth can provide more comfort in times of sorrow, more wisdom in times of distress, or more guidance in times of confusion than just spending some quiet moments with the Master, reading from His love letter to us. If you are struggling today, set aside some time to renew your strength reading His great promises.

Add your thoughts and/or prayer for the day

June 8
Psalm 22-25

Psalms 25:4-5
*"(4) Shew me thy ways, O LORD; teach me thy paths. (5)
Lead me in thy truth, and teach me: for thou art the God of
my salvation; on thee do I wait all the day."*

It is a daily process for us to know and do God's will, to walk in His Spirit, and to learn of Him. Like David we must stay teachable, knowing that the only right path is the path the Lord has chosen for us. The only real truth is that which we learn from Him. In reading the thoughts of great men of God, there is a common thread in each of their lives. They never were complacent to what they knew of God nor were they content with just learning from others. Their desire was to be taught by Christ, Himself through the scriptures. If the lessons God has for you come hard, don't give up. Just be still, meditate on them and wait until you are sure of the plan God has chosen for you.

Add your thoughts and/or prayer for the day

June 9
Psalm 26-30

Psalms 27:4
"One thing have I asked of Jehovah, that will I seek after;
That I may dwell in the house of Jehovah all the days of my
life, To behold the beauty of Jehovah, And to inquire in his
temple."

David understood the joy and beauty of just being with the Lord. It is hard to imagine a true Christian without church in their lives. Oh, it is not perfect by any stretch of the imagination, but when it is operating from the scriptures, its people are the best, its purpose is divine and God is readily seen working supernaturally through its many ministries. No other work draws people as close to the Lord as does the ministry of the church. One may condemn it and find fault, but the truth is that it is the bride of Christ and we should seek like David to dwell in the Lord's house and behold the beauty of our God and grow in His Word there. Be faithful to the house of God.

Add your thoughts and/or prayer for the day

June 10
Psalm 31-33

Psalms 32:5
"I acknowledged my sin unto thee, and mine iniquity have I not hid. I said, I will confess my transgressions unto the LORD; and thou forgavest the iniquity of my sin."

One of the greatest promises of God is that if we confess our sins, He is faithful and just to forgive us our sins and to cleanse us from all unrighteousness (1 John 1:9). The only condition is our confession. For most of us, the weight of our sin has become acceptable. We go day to day without ever spending time to really come before our Father, allowing Him to expose our sin and then truly confessing it to Him seeking His forgiveness. There is nothing like a clean slate to start the day! Spend some time today letting God free you of the weight of sin that so easily besets you.

Add your thoughts and/or prayer for the day

June 11
Psalm 34-36

Psalms 36:1-3 ESV
"(1) Transgression speaks to the wicked deep in his heart; there is no fear of God before his eyes. (2) For he flatters himself in his own eyes that his iniquity cannot be found out and hated. (3) The words of his mouth are trouble and deceit; he has ceased to act wisely and do good."

This spiritual insight from David exposes the reality of harboring sin and the mindset of those who do. The problem lies in that there is no fear of God. Over time we feel that in some way we have pulled the wool over God's eyes and gotten by with our 'secret' sin, but truth is that He is ever aware of our wickedness, and in time, it will reveal itself through our words and actions. It is best to deal with it now, confessing and repenting of it. Then get back to walking in the Spirit, enjoying communion with the Father.

Add your thoughts and/or prayer for the day

June 12
Psalm 37-39

Psalms 37:23-25
"(23) The steps of a good man are ordered by the LORD: and he delighteth in his way. (24) Though he fall, he shall not be utterly cast down: for the LORD upholdeth him with his hand. (25) I have been young, and now am old; yet have I not seen the righteous forsaken, nor his seed begging bread."

When my children were very young, they would ask if they could hold my hand. I would extend a finger and they would latch on, content to go where I was going. However, if we were approaching a street or an activity that they might lose their grip, I would then take them by the hand and hold them so if they stumbled or fell they would not be hurt. I think this verse speaks of that kind of relationship with our Heavenly Father. We stumble and even fall sometimes, but He is always there to help us up. How faithful and loving a Father we have.

Add your thoughts and/or prayer for the day

June 13
Psalm 40-44

Psalms 40:5
"Many, O LORD my God, are thy wonderful works which thou hast done, and thy thoughts which are to us-ward: they cannot be reckoned up in order unto thee: if I would declare and speak of them, they are more than can be numbered."

Sure hear a lot of complaining among God's people; something wrong with that for sure! When we stop and consider all that God has done and is doing in our lives, and in the lives of our loved ones, how can we find time to complain? Have you ever just thought of how awesome your salvation is? If the Lord saving you was the only thing He ever did for you, wasn't that more than we deserved? Come on! Stop complaining and start praising and thanking the Lord for all the blessings He has provided. Like David said, *"they are more than can be numbered."*

Add your thoughts and/or prayer for the day

June 14
Psalm 45-47

Psalm 46:10
"Be still, and know that I am God: I will be exalted among the heathen, I will be exalted in the earth."

Do you remember as a child how hard that it was to sit still? But with the Lord, that is what we need most; just be still and learn to wait. If you feel you can't be still, it is because the enemy has convinced you that you are too important to stop, but the Lord says, *"Be still!"* It is only then, when we step back from being so busy running our lives that God can take over and do what He does best, being God. That is what He says, *"Be still, and know that I am God!"* Remember this; your busy-ness is causing you to forfeit the knowledge and the peace of the One who loves you most. Be still!

Add your thoughts and/or prayer for the day

June 15
Psalm 48-50

Psalm 48:9-10
"(9) We have thought of thy lovingkindness, O God, in the midst of thy temple. (10) According to thy name, O God, so is thy praise unto the ends of the earth: thy right hand is full of righteousness."

Two attributes that David ascribes as worthy of praise are God's loving kindness and His name. His loving kindness is issued in His grace to us and every time we consider how gracious He is to us, we must praise Him! *"According to thy name"*, gives us an even greater point of praise. So our praise is not only in what He does for us, but who He is! Consider this morning who it is that we call Father. He is the Creator God, the Everlasting Father, the Prince of peace, our Redeemer, Master and Savior. Who He is prompts us to praise unto the ends of the earth! So go ahead and just let this day be a day of praising our God.

Add your thoughts and/or prayer for the day

June 16
Psalm 51-54

Psalm 51:6
"Behold, thou desirest truth in the inward parts: and in the hidden part thou shalt make me to know wisdom."

This particular verse gives the intent for which God gave us the Psalms, and that is to expose in us those things that we think are so deep inside that no one will ever know. But God knows! It is those very things that lie in our *'inward parts'* that either access God or deny access by God into our being. God wants us to worship Him in spirit and truth, but if we harbor things inside that are dishonoring to Him or us, we can see that it would hinder our worship of Him. Maybe it is time that you allow God to provide that healing in that hidden part. Give it to Him, trust in His forgiveness and healing, and find the wisdom that comes from being honest with yourself and with God.

Add your thoughts and/or prayer for the day

June 17
Psalm 55-58

Psalms 57:7-11
"(7) My heart is fixed, O God, my heart is fixed: I will sing and give praise. (8) Awake up, my glory; awake, psaltery and harp: I myself will awake early. (9) I will praise thee, O Lord, among the people: I will sing unto thee among the nations. (10) For thy mercy is great unto the heavens, and thy truth unto the clouds. (11) Be thou exalted, O God, above the heavens: let thy glory be above all the earth."

In the heat of battle, David finds his praise as he places his heart's attention back on the Master! If we allow them, our spiritual battles will take us away from the place of praise and rob us of the opportunity to glory in the presence of our Lord. If you are facing the enemy today and he seems to robbing you of your peace, it is time to get your praise on, it is time to look to your source of victory and peace. Get your heart fixed on Jesus! Awaken that heart of praise, sing, shout if need be, bask in His mercy, in His greatness and declare His authority in your life. The enemy will have no victory in your life today!

Add your thoughts and/or prayer for the day

June 18
Psalm 59-62

Psalms 59:16-17
"(16) But I will sing of thy power; yea, I will sing aloud of thy mercy in the morning: for thou hast been my defense and refuge in the day of my trouble. (17) Unto thee, O my strength, will I sing: for God is my defense, and the God of my mercy."

Many of the Psalms are an expression of an ongoing persecution of David and in these songs, David is crying out for God's help. By the end of each of them, he will acknowledge that God is faithful and will see him through the trouble. Our prayers should include supplication, asking for God's help, but they should conclude with the truth of God's faithfulness. Then we should praise Him for His power and the mercy to carry us through whatever need we might have. Our God is mighty in power and full of mercy, His desire is always toward us and He never fails in His purpose for us.

Add your thoughts and/or prayer for the day

June 19
Psalm 63-66

Psalms 63:1-2
"(1) O God, thou art my God; early will I seek thee: my soul thirsteth for thee, my flesh longeth for thee in a dry and thirsty land, where no water is; (2) To see thy power and thy glory, so as I have seen thee in the sanctuary."

Our Lord Jesus, while on earth, would find those times when He would need to be alone with the Father. There is something inside a born-again Christian that draws him to want to seek out the Lord, a connection that is only satisfied with a quiet time, one-on-one with the Father. In these verses, David reveals the passion for a moment with God that will only be satisfied by seeing God in His power and glory. David refers to it as a sanctuary. Do you have such a place? A quiet serene place where you, alone with God, find a satisfaction that can only be supplied by your Father? If not, you need to. You will find Him waiting on you there.

Add your thoughts and/or prayer for the day

June 20
Psalm 67-70

Psalms 68:7-8
"(7) O God, when thou wentest forth before thy people, when thou didst march through the wilderness (8) The earth shook, the heavens also dropped at the presence of God: even Sinai itself was moved at the presence of God, the God of Israel."

The evidence of God's protection and providence for Israel as they traveled by the Lord's divine guidance gave them witness to the greatness of their God. When we will give heed to the Lord's leadership and allow Him to be complete ruler of our lives, that same sovereignty is ours to witness as well. All of nature bows before our God and puts itself at His disposal to accomplish His mighty plans. At His voice, mountains will be moved out of place and the heavens will bow at His presence. That's our God! What is it that worries your soul today? Our Father is big enough and powerful enough to handle whatever you face. Hold His hand and walk through it!

Add your thoughts and/or prayer for the day

June 21
Psalms 71-74

Psalm 73:24-26
"(24) Thou shalt guide me with thy counsel, and afterward receive me to glory. (25) Whom have I in heaven but thee? and there is none upon earth that I desire beside thee. (26) My flesh and my heart faileth: but God is the strength of my heart, and my portion for ever."

David, in this Psalm at first, like so many, complains that he sees the unrighteous seemingly being blessed with all kinds of worldly blessings. He finally realizes that what he has in God is so much better than all the riches of this earth. If you have been guilty of envying those who have the world's riches, then stop and realize all you have in Christ; His counsel, the promise of His glory, just to know that you walk in His presence. Your strength as a child of God is not found in earthly goods, but in your relationship with the Almighty. Find your joy, your strength, your prosperity in Him.

Add your thoughts and/or prayer for the day

June 22
Psalms 75-78

Psalm 78:5-7
"(5) For he established a testimony in Jacob, and appointed a law in Israel, which he commanded our fathers, that they should make them known to their children: (6) That the generation to come might know them, even the children which should be born; who should arise and declare them to their children: (7) That they might set their hope in God, and not forget the works of God, but keep his commandments"

God has commanded that fathers teach their children the works of God. The children of Israel continually failed to do this and God was continually chastening them because of it. Today it is reported that only 15% of high school children have attended church. We need to get back to teaching our children about God, instead of all the other stuff we spend so much money and time trying to 'give them what we did not have'. What we had was the Lord and He is enough!

Add your thoughts and/or prayer for the day

June 23
Psalms 79-83

Psalm 79:4-6
"(4) *We are become a reproach to our neighbours, a scorn and derision to them that are round about us. (5) How long, LORD? wilt thou be angry for ever? shall thy jealousy burn like fire? (6) Pour out thy wrath upon the heathen that have not known thee, and upon the kingdoms that have not called upon thy name.*"

David, like many of the Christians of today, complain to God about the state of our society and how the world is taking advantage of those who are God's children. He begs God to do something to the "heathen" so He would be glorified. The problem with that is God has given us the command to bring glory to His name. Instead of asking God to purge the world of sin, we might do best to seek forgiveness for our sin of not living as a witness for Him. Be careful not to get sucked into the mindset that we are victims; we are not. We are, however, the recipient God's chastisement for our own disobedience and in need of revival.

Add your thoughts and/or prayer for the day

June 24
Psalms 84-88

Psalm 86:10-12
"(10) For thou art great, and doest wondrous things: thou art God alone. (11) Teach me thy way, O LORD; I will walk in thy truth: unite my heart to fear thy name. (12) I will praise thee, O Lord my God, with all my heart: and I will glorify thy name for evermore."

How awesome is our God! So much so, that it is a never-ending lesson for us to learn of His character, His ability, His love and mercy. The more we come to know of Him, the more we stand in awe of Him. The closer we get to Him, the more we realize how much more there is to learn of Him. That is why the psalmist says he will glorify the name of the Lord for evermore. It will take that long for us to examine and experience the awesomeness of our Lord!

Add your thoughts and/or prayer for the day

June 25
Psalms 89-92

Psalms 90:2
"Before the mountains were brought forth, or ever thou hadst formed the earth and the world, even from everlasting to everlasting, thou art God."

A child will ask the question that all will ponder, "If God created everything, who created God?" There is a truth that everyone will have to acknowledge, that before anything existed, something or someone had to exist. In other words, something or someone has to be eternal. It goes beyond our human understanding, because we are finite and mortal, yet we cannot escape its truth. When we accept this truth by faith, it is then that we can begin to learn of this awesome God who created us and even now seeks a relationship with us. Even that is beyond our human understanding, that the eternal creator God would desire a relationship with us. Yet it is true! This God loves you!

Add your thoughts and/or prayer for the day

June 26
Psalms 93-96

Psalm 96:1-5
*"(1) O sing unto the LORD a new song: sing unto the LORD,
all the earth. (2) Sing unto the LORD, bless his name; shew
forth his salvation from day to day. (3) Declare his glory
among the heathen, his wonders among all people. (4) For
the LORD is great, and greatly to be praised: he is to be
feared above all gods. (5) For all the gods of the nations are
idols: but the LORD made the heavens."*

There are just not enough words to express the love of
God, like the hymn says, "Could we with ink the ocean fill,
And were the skies of parchment made, Were every stalk
on earth a quill, And every man a scribe by trade; To write
the love of God above, Would drain the ocean dry; Nor
could the scroll contain the whole, Though stretched from
sky to sky."

Add your thoughts and/or prayer for the day

June 27
Psalms 97-101

Psalm 100:2-4
"(2) Serve the LORD with gladness: come before his presence with singing. (3) Know ye that the LORD he is God: it is he that hath made us, and not we ourselves; we are his people, and the sheep of his pasture. (4) Enter into his gates with thanksgiving, and into his courts with praise: be thankful unto him, and bless his name."

Serving the Lord in any way should be one of the most exciting and exhilarating tasks a person could be called to do. It is when we are working with our Father side-by-side, that we come to know Him on that deep intimate level. It is then that we feel and understand His passion and love for us. So come on! Get your serve on and serve the Lord with all your heart. Get involved, sell out, jump in with both feet; it is the adventure of a lifetime!

Add your thoughts and/or prayer for the day

June 28
Psalms 102-104

Psalm 104:31-34

"*(31) The glory of the LORD shall endure for ever: the LORD shall rejoice in his works. (32) He looketh on the earth, and it trembleth: he toucheth the hills, and they smoke. (33) I will sing unto the LORD as long as I live: I will sing praise to my God while I have my being. (34) My meditation of him shall be sweet: I will be glad in the LORD.*"

How can anyone spend any time looking at the wonderful creation of God and not just get overwhelmed with the awesome beauty and wonder of His handiwork. Our Father is worthy of every song, every prayer of praise, every action of love we direct toward Him. Never let anything or anyone rob you of the joy and gladness we find in Him. May your meditation of Him today be ever so sweet!

Add your thoughts and/or prayer for the day

June 29
Psalms 105-107

Psalms 106:36-41 ESV
"(36) *They served their idols, which became a snare to them.
(37) They sacrificed their sons and their daughters to the
demons; (38) they poured out innocent blood, the blood of
their sons and daughters, whom they sacrificed to the idols of
Canaan, and the land was polluted with blood. (39) Thus
they became unclean by their acts, and played the whore in
their deeds. (40) Then the anger of the LORD was kindled
against his people, and he abhorred his heritage; (41) he
gave them into the hand of the nations, so that those who
hated them ruled over them.*"

God is a loving, merciful and grace-filled Sovereign, but He
is holy, just and jealous as well, terms we many times
forget. Beware, dear child of God, in this age of tolerance
and political correctness, that you don't allow yourself to
be lured into believing that God has softened His desire
for His own to be a chosen generation, a royal priesthood,
an holy nation, a peculiar people. If He demanded this
obedience of Israel and would bring judgment on them for
their disbelief, He can and will do the same on His bride,
the church.

Add your thoughts and/or prayer for the day

June 30
Psalms 108-111

Psalm 109:28-30
"(28) Let them curse, but bless thou: when they arise, let them be ashamed; but let thy servant rejoice. (29) Let mine adversaries be clothed with shame, and let them cover themselves with their own confusion, as with a mantle. (30) I will greatly praise the LORD with my mouth; yea, I will praise him among the multitude."

As we approach the end times, the enemies of Christ and His followers grow stronger and stronger. Our answer to them must still be the love of Christ. Although they may never come to know the truth of our Lord, and our continual praise of Him only confuses them, it is our responsibility to continue to be the Lord's hands, His feet and His heart. It may appear that we are losing at times, but we know in the end, our Lord wins it all!

Add your thoughts and/or prayer for the day

July 1
Psalms 112-115

Psalms 115:1-4
"(1) Not unto us, O LORD, not unto us, but unto thy name give glory, for thy mercy, and for thy truth's sake. (2) Wherefore should the heathen say, Where is now their God? (3) But our God is in the heavens: he hath done whatsoever he hath pleased. (4) Their idols are silver and gold, the work of men's hands."

We know, as God's children, that it is God who deserves all glory, not man. The lost world confuses this and thinks it is all about man, which is why they will question God when things don't go as they would have planned. Their security is in the things of this world, the things that cannot last and in the end, will always fail them. But our God is above all! He is eternal, merciful, and full of truth; He cannot fail! Be careful, dear child of God. that you don't get too attached to what the world seeks as god. Seek only to serve and honor the One who deserves all our praise.

Add your thoughts and/or prayer for the day

July 2
Psalms 116-118

Psalm 116:1-2
"(1) I love the LORD, because he hath heard my voice and my supplications. (2) Because he hath inclined his ear unto me, therefore will I call upon him as long as I live."

Prayer is simply a conversation with God. It is one of the most powerful tools the Lord has given to His children. In Christ, we have been given access to come boldly unto the throne of grace that we may obtain mercy, and find grace to help in time of need. Do not ever forget when you bow your head and just say, "Father", that the Creator of the universe, the eternal, all powerful sovereign God of heaven replies back to you, "yes, my child". As the Lord has told us, pray always!

Add your thoughts and/or prayer for the day

July 3
Psalm 119

Psalm 119:133-135
"(133) *Order my steps in thy word: and let not any iniquity have dominion over me. (134) Deliver me from the oppression of man: so will I keep thy precepts. (135) Make thy face to shine upon thy servant; and teach me thy statutes.*"

There is great comfort, encouragement, strength and wisdom to be found in God's word. The problem is that we spend so little time in it, that when we need something, we don't know where to find it, but it is there. Enjoy and be encouraged by the devotions, lessons and sermons of those who present the Word, but never let that be a substitute for your own personal study of God's word. The Bible is God's love letter to YOU. Find His special message for you each day from reading its pages.

Add your thoughts and/or prayer for the day

July 4
Happy Independence Day from the Newtons.
Let's pray for America!
Psalm 120-125

Psalms 124:8
*"Our help is in the name of the LORD, who made
heaven and earth."*

As Americans, we celebrate today as our day of independence and we have been blessed to live in this great nation. As now we face times of seeming tyranny, we should remember that every nation rises and falls under God's watchful eye. Like Benjamin Franklin said, "I have lived, Sir, a long time, and the longer I live, the more convincing proofs I see of this truth -- that God Governs in the affairs of men. And if a sparrow cannot fall to the ground without his notice, is it probable that an empire can rise without his aid?" Pray for our country and pray that we, as God's children, will stand firm upon the principles of His word.

Add your thoughts and/or prayer for the day

July 5
Psalms 126-131

Psalm 130:3-6
"(3) If thou, LORD, shouldest mark iniquities, O Lord, who shall stand? (4) But there is forgiveness with thee, that thou mayest be feared. (5) I wait for the LORD, my soul doth wait, and in his word do I hope. (6) My soul waiteth for the Lord more than they that watch for the morning: I say, more than they that watch for the morning."

If we could not find full forgiveness for our sin in Christ's sacrifice for us on Calvary, we would live in a constant sickening, unhealthy fear of what might happen next. But the fact that God has offered us a complete pardon for sin and graced us with His Spirit to confirm our position as a child of God, we now live in a holy, reverent fear of how awesome our Father is; which allows us to patiently wait and watch for our Lord with loving anticipation for His appearing.

Add your thoughts and/or prayer for the day

<u>July 6</u>
Psalms 132-135

Psalm 135:1-3
"(1) Praise ye the LORD. Praise ye the name of the LORD; praise him, O ye servants of the LORD. (2) Ye that stand in the house of the LORD, in the courts of the house of our God, (3) Praise the LORD; for the LORD is good: sing praises unto his name; for it is pleasant."

Today, like every day, should be a day of praise! For those of us who serve the Lord with our lives, we find so much about our Lord that promotes our praise of Him. His name alone is an unending source of praise. It is in His name that we find power, strength, love, grace, and mercy! In His name, we find our salvation and our security for living. Truth is that there is nothing about our Lord that doesn't deserve praise; so go ahead, praise your awesome Lord!

Add your thoughts and/or prayer for the day

July 7
Psalms 136-140

Psalm 139:1-4
*"(1) O LORD, thou hast searched me, and known me. (2)
Thou knowest my downsitting and mine uprising, thou
understandest my thought afar off. (3) Thou compassest my
path and my lying down, and art acquainted with all my
ways. (4) For there is not a word in my tongue, but, lo, O
LORD, thou knowest it altogether."*

What a wonderful Psalm! The whole of it expresses the
Lord's unfettered love and involvement in each of our lives.
His concern is for all of His created ones. There is no place
we can go to escape His presence. Just the mere fact that
He knows us intimately from the time of our conception
and throughout our lives, like the psalmist says is too
wonderful and above our understanding.

Add your thoughts and/or prayer for the day

July 8
Psalms 141-145

Psalm 141:3
*"Set a watch, O LORD, before my mouth; keep the
door of my lips."*

Our words can be used by God to bring comfort, encouragement and even victory to the hearers. However, our words can be used by the enemy and be more devastating than a blow to the face or a gunshot wound to the stomach, because they go right to the heart. We speak of physical abuse as being disabling. But the truth is that more harm is caused by verbal abuse that creates lasting scars - scars that can hinder a person from ever succeeding in life. If we are people who are saved by grace, then our words should be filled with grace. Let's work on that today. Think before you speak.

Add your thoughts and/or prayer for the day

Psalm 150:1-6
"(1) Praise ye the LORD. Praise God in his sanctuary: praise him in the firmament of his power. (2) Praise him for his mighty acts: praise him according to his excellent greatness. (3) Praise him with the sound of the trumpet: praise him with the psaltery and harp. (4) Praise him with the timbrel and dance: praise him with stringed instruments and organs. (5) Praise him upon the loud cymbals: praise him upon the high sounding cymbals. (6) Let every thing that hath breath praise the LORD. Praise ye the LORD."

The challenge today is to find something in everything you do to praise the Lord! Don't get so caught up in the activity that you forget to see God's involvement in it, from the smallest to the greatest act, from the most insignificant to the most profound. Praise the Lord!

Add your thoughts and/or prayer for the day

Proverbs 1-3

Proverbs 1:28-30
"(28) Then shall they call upon me, but I will not answer;
they shall seek me early, but they shall not find me: (29) For
that they hated knowledge, and did not choose the fear of the
LORD: (30) They would none of my counsel: they despised
all my reproof."

When people consistently push God and His wisdom and guidance away, they will pay a regretful toll when times of trouble come and they need Him. God is faithful, but God is just, and the scripture is clear that He will chasten those He loves. Pray for our nation as we have allowed this country to turn its back on God. We have not stood up for His righteousness in our choices for our leaders, and now we see the unfruitful works of darkness taking over. Don't be surprised when we call upon God for help and He refuses to answer.

Add your thoughts and/or prayer for the day

July 11
Proverbs 4-6

Proverbs 4:25-27
"(25) Let thine eyes look right on, and let thine eyelids look straight before thee. (26) Ponder the path of thy feet, and let all thy ways be established. (27) Turn not to the right hand nor to the left: remove thy foot from evil."

Paul said in Ephesians 5:15 to walk 'circumspectly', which means to carefully place each step with care and purpose. Here Solomon gives advice to keep your attention upon your path, don't stray from it and place each step with purpose. How much of our life is carelessly wasted, when we spend it following after sin's allurement when we could be enjoying the blessings of walking in fellowship with the love of our Father. Dear child of God, watch your step!

Add your thoughts and/or prayer for the day

Proverbs 8:12-14 ESV
"(12) I, wisdom, dwell with prudence, and I find knowledge and discretion. (13) The fear of the LORD is hatred of evil. Pride and arrogance and the way of evil and perverted speech I hate. (14) I have counsel and sound wisdom; I have insight; I have strength."

Solomon in this proverb speaks of wisdom and explains that in it we will find truth and guidance. We will also realize the folly of our own self-will in seeking only to supply our own gratification when there are much greater things to obtain in this life. Wisdom will bring us to that holy reverence called the fear of the Lord. It will awaken our senses to the evil in pride, arrogance and promoting of self. It is obvious that self and selfishness cannot dwell with wisdom and the fear of the Lord. As James reminds us, *"If any of you lacks wisdom, let him ask God, who gives generously to all without reproach, and it will be given him."* - Seek wisdom!

Add your thoughts and/or prayer for the day

<u>July 13</u>
Proverbs 10-12

Proverbs 10:29-30
"(29) The way of the LORD is strength to the upright: but destruction shall be to the workers of iniquity. (30) The righteous shall never be removed: but the wicked shall not inhabit the earth."

Righteousness edifies and builds, while works of unrighteousness destroy and provide no hope. Atheism does nothing to build or promote a person. Without God, what hope does anyone have to offer, but with the truth of God and His word we find healing, strength, power and hope! If we follow unrighteousness, we can expect to find hopelessness, sorrow, and defeat. If we follow the Lord, on the other hand, we find peace, purpose, and victory. You have the right to choose. Which one makes more sense?

<u>Add your thoughts and/or prayer for the day</u>

July 14
Proverbs 13-15

Proverbs 14:26-27
"(26) In the fear of the LORD is strong confidence: and his children shall have a place of refuge. (27) The fear of the LORD is a fountain of life, to depart from the snares of death."

Some wonder at the fear of the Lord. Is it to be scared of God? No way! This fear is a reverent fear, an awe of God's holiness and ability. This fear is to respect our Father and the position He takes in our lives. It is to give Him the honor that He deserves. This kind of reverent awe expressed as the fear of the Lord gives us that confidence that our Father can do anything and we find great peace in knowing He is in charge.

Add your thoughts and/or prayer for the day

July 15
Proverbs 16-18

Proverbs 17:17
"A friend loveth at all times, and a brother is born for adversity."

Friendship is truly a gift from God! God leads people in and out of our lives throughout our lives, each leaving a print upon our soul valuable in making us into the person God wants us to be. But there are a few, and sometimes could be only one, that steps over from the friend to a brother category. As much as friendship is awesome, to have them become a brother is incredible! You realize this person has or would have stood with you, no matter the circumstance. They pray with you. They are always just a call away and are ready at a moment's notice to render what aid they can. Thank God for our friendships, but consider it God's great gift when the friend becomes a brother!

Add your thoughts and/or prayer for the day

July 16
Proverbs 19-21

Proverbs 20:6-7
"(6) Most men will proclaim every one his own goodness: but a faithful man who can find? (7) The just man walketh in his integrity: his children are blessed after him."

Two of the most important character qualities of a person of faith would be faithfulness and integrity. Both of which seem harder and harder to find. The Bible says that in the end times, men will be lovers of themselves more than lovers of God and truly that has become the problem today. For most, the only thing they can be faithful to is doing only what they want to do and integrity has been replaced with greed and selfishness. Consider today your faithfulness and your integrity, especially when it comes to being involved with the Lord's work.

Add your thoughts and/or prayer for the day

Proverbs 23:24-26
"(24) The father of the righteous shall greatly rejoice: and he that begetteth a wise child shall have joy of him. (25) Thy father and thy mother shall be glad, and she that bare thee shall rejoice. (26) My son, give me thine heart, and let thine eyes observe my ways."

The proverb is two-fold. To the parent, we should spend a lot of time teaching and training our children in the ways of righteousness. To the child who is making their own decisions, they should weigh carefully their decisions as to the effect it has on others, especially their parents. Children who have made the decision to walk in the way of the Lord bring so much joy to their parents, while the wayward child making poor decisions brings sleepless nights and broken hearts to theirs. How have your decisions affected your parents or your children?

Add your thoughts and/or prayer for the day

July 18
Proverbs 25-28

Proverbs 27:6
"Faithful are the wounds of a friend; but the kisses of an enemy are deceitful."

We all love flattery, the bolstering of our egos. But thank goodness for the true friend that will bring us back to earth with a reality check, always done in love, but always in a way that makes us realize that God's involvement through us is so much more important than what we supposedly do for Him or others. Be careful, dear child of God, that you appreciate the friend who may sometimes leave a wound by pulling our heads out of the sky or deflating our big heads. Those wounds will heal, but false pride or a haughty spirit will only dishonor our self and our Father.

Add your thoughts and/or prayer for the day

Proverbs 31:10-12
"(10) Who can find a virtuous woman? for her price is far above rubies. (11) The heart of her husband doth safely trust in her, so that he shall have no need of spoil. (12) She will do him good and not evil all the days of her life."

A home that is built around virtue is one where the husband and wife live in a harmony that can only be found by the Spirit of God leading them. The husband serving his wife and the wife serving her husband, and both of them enjoying having their needs met. When this gets out of balance by one seeking selfish desires, the marriage suffers and the harmony is lost to confusion and contention. Serving is the highest priority of a godly man or woman.

Add your thoughts and/or prayer for the day

July 20
Ecclesiastes 1-4

Ecclesiastes 4:9-10
"(9) Two are better than one; because they have a good reward for their labour. (10) For if they fall, the one will lift up his fellow: but woe to him that is alone when he falleth; for he hath not another to help him up."

God, in creating man, never intended for him to be alone. In fact, the first thing in God's creation that God deemed not good was that man was alone. We need each other! No matter how frustrating it may be sometimes, we need others. Jesus taught that we should love our neighbors as ourselves. Sometimes it seems easier to just ignore or even hide from others, but instead we need to reach out, in God's love, to be a part of each other's lives. Stretch yourself to reach out to someone else today.

Add your thoughts and/or prayer for the day

July 21
Ecclesiastes 5-8

Ecclesiastes 8:17
*"Then I beheld all the work of God, that a man cannot find
out the work that is done under the sun: because though a
man labour to seek it out, yet he shall not find it; yea further;
though a wise man think to know it, yet shall he not be
able to find it."*

The unsearchable depth of the wisdom, might, and ability of God makes Him God! No matter how far we go in our research and study of God and His work, there is always something else to learn. A student of the word of God finds this to be so true, yet it is not frustrating, but instead intriguing and fascinating. The living Word of God teaching us about the living God of the Word. Keep digging, my friend, the knowledge of Him is as wonderful as it is unfathomable.

Add your thoughts and/or prayer for the day

July 22
Ecclesiastes 9-12

Ecclesiastes 12:13-14
"(13) Let us hear the conclusion of the whole matter: Fear God, and keep his commandments: for this is the whole duty of man. (14) For God shall bring every work into judgment, with every secret thing, whether it be good, or whether it be evil."

After considering all the avenues of life, Solomon concludes that all that really matters is our relationship to God and how we treat others. Isn't that what the Lord said when asked what the greatest commandment was? Love God! Love others! If we would consistently live by that rule, then God will take care of the rest. Leave judgment with the Lord, He will always get it right.

Add your thoughts and/or prayer for the day

July 23
Song of Solomon 1-4

Song of Solomon 1:2-3
"(2) Let him kiss me with the kisses of his mouth: for thy love is better than wine. (3) Because of the savour of thy good ointments thy name is as ointment poured forth, therefore do the virgins love thee."

This beautiful love story starts with a kiss. It is the kiss of a wedding ceremony sealing the covenant between two people. The Lord gives us this story to demonstrate the relationship the Lord has with his people, as a groom to his bride. It is in this relationship that we are given His name and become one with him. The Lord wants us to understand that His love for us is not just simple, superficial, puppy love, but His love for us is deep, intimate, supernatural love. If you are one of His, then know and respond to the intimacy of His love.

Add your thoughts and/or prayer for the day

July 24
Song of Solomon 5-8

Song of Solomon 8:7 ESV
"Many waters cannot quench love, neither can floods drown it. If a man offered for love all the wealth of his house, he would be utterly despised."

Throughout this story is the importance of love. Here, the writer explains that there is no substitute for love. To try to offer anything in exchange for love would be *'utterly despised'*. In our relationship with the Lord, His desire is for us to respond to Him out of love. When we act out of His love, the actions will be pure and unconditional. When we try to prove our love with self motivating actions, with the desire to in some way get rewarded for our love, it only cheapens it. Just be in love with Christ, allow His love to be the resource for your actions and the actions that follow will come easily.

Add your thoughts and/or prayer for the day

Isaiah 1:16-17
"(16) Wash you, make you clean; put away the evil of your doings from before mine eyes; cease to do evil; (17) Learn to do well; seek judgment, relieve the oppressed, judge the fatherless, plead for the widow."

A call to repentance! Israel had grown proud, idolatrous and self-willed. Now God sends the prophet to call them back to true worship. It all begins with a repentive spirit. We need to remain humble before the Lord, realizing that there is no good in us except that which we find in Christ. The Lord will do the cleaning, but we must make the decision for repentance. A reminder today, as you start the day, wash up and then make the decision to turn from sin through the strength you will find in the Lord.

Add your thoughts and/or prayer for the day

Isaiah 5:21-23
"(21) Woe unto them that are wise in their own eyes, and prudent in their own sight! (22) Woe unto them that are mighty to drink wine, and men of strength to mingle strong drink: (23) Which justify the wicked for reward, and take away the righteousness of the righteous from him!"

The prophet is warning Israel of the things that will bring judgment against them. This woe is one that is seen more and more, men who are wrapped up in their own pride, considering themselves real men and women of the world, because of their ability to consume alcoholic beverages. What is worse is that they are not satisfied with making this lifestyle for themselves; they have to drag anyone that wants to befriend them into it as well. God is looking for real men and women of God that can walk in holiness and stand with Him against the destructive powers of Satan. Sometimes it will call on us to stand alone, so then stand!

Add your thoughts and/or prayer for the day

July 27
Isaiah 7-9

Isaiah 9:6
*"For unto us a child is born, unto us a son is given: and the
government shall be upon his shoulder: and his name shall be
called Wonderful, Counsellor, The mighty God, The
everlasting Father, The Prince of Peace."*

Although at the time of his life and death, most did not
see Jesus as the prophet describes, since that time we
have seen Him described by all these titles. One day the
Lord will return and establish a kingdom here on earth for
a thousand years. What a wonderful truth to know that in
all the turmoil that the world is enduring now, that there is
coming a time when the world will enjoy complete peace
under the reign of the Prince of Peace. Did you know that
you don't have to wait to enjoy that awesome peace? The
Prince of Peace who rules your heart can provide peace in
the time of trials right now.

Add your thoughts and/or prayer for the day

July 28
Isaiah 10-12

Isaiah 12:2
"Behold, God is my salvation; I will trust, and not be afraid: for the LORD JEHOVAH is my strength and my song; he also is become my salvation."

A song for this day! No matter the circumstance you may face, no matter the hardship or difficulty that life has presented, today make this your praise. The Lord has not forgotten you; He is still your salvation. Put your full trust in His ability, knowing that He is your sovereign Lord. Cease from any fear that may have seeped into your thoughts and fill that space with His unfathomable peace. The Lord God, who can take the sins of the whole world and in one precise moment in time, take those sins and provide complete forgiveness for them for all of eternity, can take care of you!

Add your thoughts and/or prayer for the day

Isaiah 14:16-17
"(16) They that see thee shall narrowly look upon thee, and consider thee, saying, Is this the man that made the earth to tremble, that did shake kingdoms; (17) That made the world as a wilderness, and destroyed the cities thereof; that opened not the house of his prisoners?"

These verses speak of Lucifer, the Devil. When we finally see him, it will surprise us that there is nothing so special or overpowering about him. Yet he is credited with all the evil in the world today. Truth is, his job is easy, so easy that in the history of time, he has never changed his tactics of tempting with the things we see, the things we want and just our sinful pride. So we are warned to be sober and vigilant against this adversary, but in the end, he loses and we are the victors. Resist him and he will flee from you, draw near to God and live as a victor instead of a victim.

Add your thoughts and/or prayer for the day

July 30
Isaiah 16-18

Isaiah 17:7-8
"(7) At that day shall a man look to his Maker, and his eyes shall have respect to the Holy One of Israel. (8) And he shall not look to the altars, the work of his hands, neither shall respect that which his fingers have made, either the groves, or the images."

There is coming a day when men will no longer be concerned with all the material things that have so captivated their attention in this day. They will realize that God is the one who deserves all his attention, all his respect. Now that will be a glorious day for those who have spent their lives loving and serving the Lord, but for those who have put everything ahead of the Lord, it will be a day of reckoning. Which will it be for you? It is never too late to start investing your time and energy in the one who loves you so much.

Add your thoughts and/or prayer for the day

<u>July 31</u>
Isaiah 19-21

Isaiah 19:24-25
"(24) In that day shall Israel be the third with Egypt and with Assyria, even a blessing in the midst of the land: (25) Whom the LORD of hosts shall bless, saying, Blessed be Egypt my people, and Assyria the work of my hands, and Israel mine inheritance."

"In that day" speaks of a future event, usually to the return of Christ. There is coming a day when in the Middle East, these countries which are in war today will worship together at the feet of Jesus. As you read this particular chapter concerning Egypt, which is primarily a Muslim country now, you find that it will come to know the Lord as God and their worship will be turned from their false religion to the eternal living God of scripture. Jesus is coming again! In that day, all will worship the one true God. What a promise; what a truth! He deserves our worship now.

Add your thoughts and/or prayer for the day

August 1
Isaiah 22-24

Isaiah 23:8-9
"(8) Who hath taken this counsel against Tyre, the crowning city, whose merchants are princes, whose traffickers are the honourable of the earth? (9) The LORD of hosts hath purposed it, to stain the pride of all glory, and to bring into contempt all the honourable of the earth."

In our day and time, there are many that think they are above the law, creating empires around them hoping to secure their fortunes. They walk with such pride and arrogance honored by the world's standards, but the Lord will only allow this self-willed pride to last only so long until He brings it down. God is God alone, He is the absolute ruler and no one has gained anything without His purpose or His provision. Our Lord will be held in honor when all else has failed.

Add your thoughts and/or prayer for the day

August 2
Isaiah 25-27

Isaiah 26:3-4
"(3) Thou wilt keep him in perfect peace, whose mind is stayed on thee: because he trusteth in thee. (4) Trust ye in the LORD for ever: for in the LORD JEHOVAH is everlasting strength"

Where do you find your peace? Real peace is not found in a place, but in a person, the Lord. The world has none to offer, their peace is only temporal, short lived, but God's peace is rich, full and lasting. The peace of God is found as we learn to depend upon Him and not ourselves. The peace of God is found when our attention is focused on Him and not our circumstances. The peace of God is found when we have come to the end our strength and turn to find that His strength is more than enough to see us through. Keep your thoughts centered on the Lord and you'll find the peace you've been looking for.

Add your thoughts and/or prayer for the day

Isaiah 30:9-11
"(9) That this is a rebellious people, lying children, children that will not hear the law of the LORD: (10) Which say to the seers, See not; and to the prophets, Prophesy not unto us right things, speak unto us smooth things, prophesy deceits: (11) Get you out of the way, turn aside out of the path, cause the Holy One of Israel to cease from before us."

Pollsters tell us now that people don't want to hear about the death, burial and resurrection of Jesus, they want to hear messages that are more 'relevant' to their needs. Preachers who once stood upon the Word of God, never apologizing for its content, are being replaced by slick wordsters that can put just enough Bible-spin to their message to satisfy those who don't know better. Instead of producing the conviction of an unholy people before a holy God, their message just makes everyone feel good about themselves. Better be careful! In these last days, the Lord warned that even the elect can be misguided.

Add your thoughts and/or prayer for the day

August 4
Isaiah 31-33

Isaiah 33:5-6
"(5) The LORD is exalted; for he dwelleth on high: he hath filled Zion with judgment and righteousness. (6) And wisdom and knowledge shall be the stability of thy times, and strength of salvation: the fear of the LORD is his treasure."

Wisdom, knowledge and strength of salvation; these are the true blessings of the children of God. Not that we produce these in and of ourselves, for we cannot, but the Lord produces these in us through the work of His Spirit. Wisdom is the ability to use what God has given us to find the truth in every situation. Knowledge is ability to receive and understand the facts of God's attributes. And the strength of our salvation is that confidence we find through the indwelling Spirit that no matter the situation, we are always the children of God. In all of this, we come to know our Lord and there is a reverent awe that consumes us, this is the fear of the Lord.

Add your thoughts and/or prayer for the day

August 5
Isaiah 34-36

Isaiah 35:8-10
"(8) And an highway shall be there, and a way, and it shall be called The way of holiness; the unclean shall not pass over it; but it shall be for those: the wayfaring men, though fools, shall not err therein. (9) No lion shall be there, nor any ravenous beast shall go up thereon, it shall not be found there; but the redeemed shall walk there: (10) And the ransomed of the LORD shall return, and come to Zion with songs and everlasting joy upon their heads: they shall obtain joy and gladness, and sorrow and sighing shall flee away."

No matter what life may be dishing out to you today, stay faithful, walk the way of holiness. These times of conflict and confusion will end, and then our rest continues in perfect peace. Stay true, faithful, committed, for the Captain of your life has plotted the course and He will see you safely home.

Add your thoughts and/or prayer for the day

August 6
Isaiah 37-40

Isaiah 40:17-18
"(17) All nations before him are as nothing; and they are counted to him less than nothing, and vanity. (18) To whom then will ye liken God? or what likeness will ye compare unto him?"

Men seek power. To be the ruler of a nation seems to be the ultimate goal. Governments think too highly of themselves, because in God's eyes they are nothing. God is the one who allows powers that be. Not one of them has come to power without His knowledge and none can exist except He allows it. Our Lord is completely sovereign and incomparable! He is above all things, rules over all things, created all things. The idea that we think we can ascribe Him any position is ludicrous, because He is above all those positions. Check your faith; is it in men and their ability to govern or in the Lord and His ability to rule?

Add your thoughts and/or prayer for the day

August 7
Isaiah 41-43

Isaiah 43:1
"But now thus saith the LORD that created thee, O Jacob, and he that formed thee, O Israel, Fear not: for I have redeemed thee, I have called thee by thy name; thou art mine."

This whole text that we read this morning is a testimony of God's love for Israel. As we see this little nation fight for existence with all the nations that are so much larger and so many who have allied against it, yet it stands strong, proud and resilient. How? Because God has a special place in His heart for this people and through all their struggles the Lord has kept it together. Why? Well, that is because the Lord sovereignly chose it to be a people He would use to demonstrate His love and blessing upon. What is really awesome is that it is through this nation that God promised to bless all people and He fulfilled that promise in Jesus Christ who came as Savior, not only for the Jew, but for all men.

Add your thoughts and/or prayer for the day

August 8
Isaiah 44-47

Isaiah 46:9-10
"(9) Remember the former things of old: for I am God, and there is none else; I am God, and there is none like me, (10) Declaring the end from the beginning, and from ancient times the things that are not yet done, saying, My counsel shall stand, and I will do all my pleasure"

"Remember" God says! Why should the Lord have to remind us of who He is? In our daily living, we fail to acknowledge His involvement so much of the time that before long, we really think we are in control. We move God off the throne of our life and begin to take on the role of god for ourselves. Then when things aren't turning out so well we cry foul, as if it is God's fault. God has a purpose for your life and everything that He allows into your life; you just can't see it when you are sitting on the throne that was designed for Him. Maybe it's time for a change. Maybe it's time that you let Him be King of your life.

Add your thoughts and/or prayer for the day

August 9
Isaiah 48-50

Isaiah 50:11
"Behold, all ye that kindle a fire, that compass yourselves about with sparks: walk in the light of your fire, and in the sparks that ye have kindled. This shall ye have of mine hand; ye shall lie down in sorrow."

What a promise the Lord gives and one that we see in our lives over and over again. If we choose to walk in the light of our own fire, our own light, the Lord promises that we will come to the end of each day only to lie down in sorrow. How amazing it is that we continue to run in our own energy and our own wisdom, always running out of steam and coming to the wrong conclusions. Then praying at the end of the day, "Lord, what went wrong?", when all the time the Lord and our Savior is living in us to give us strength, wisdom, encouragement and guidance. Seek the Lord's fire, the promise it offers will not leave you disappointed.

Add your thoughts and/or prayer for the day

August 10
Isaiah 51-53

Isaiah 52:7
"How beautiful upon the mountains are the feet of him that bringeth good tidings, that publisheth peace; that bringeth good tidings of good, that publisheth salvation; that saith unto Zion, Thy God reigneth!"

How are your feet looking these days? Don't you just love the fact that the Lord really does pay attention to the things we do and say? The Lord has made us to glorify Him, which is our sole purpose in this life. How are we to do that? In everything we do, and especially in how we communicate with others. As His children, we have the greatest news that anyone could ever hear; God loves them, Jesus died for them and there is salvation in Him. So according to Isaiah, how are your feet looking these days? Beautiful? If not, then look around you at all the people you could be telling the good news!

Add your thoughts and/or prayer for the day

August 11
Isaiah 54-56

Isaiah 55:6-7
"(6) Seek ye the LORD while he may be found, call ye upon him while he is near: (7) Let the wicked forsake his way, and the unrighteous man his thoughts: and let him return unto the LORD, and he will have mercy upon him; and to our God, for he will abundantly pardon."

It is required as men that we commit ourselves to seeking the Lord, to calling on Him, and to turning from our sin. Amazingly enough, people don't get this. They have it in their thoughts that God is supposed to do the seeking, the calling and forsaking of sin. God will do His part of forgiving and offering pardon, but we must do our part. God will not violate the free will He has given you because it is in that free will we can demonstrate our love, loyalty, and commitment to Him. Do your part; God will not fail to keep His end of the relationship!

Add your thoughts and/or prayer for the day

August 12
Isaiah 57-59

Isaiah 57:15
"For thus saith the high and lofty One that inhabiteth eternity, whose name is Holy; I dwell in the high and holy place, with him also that is of a contrite and humble spirit, to revive the spirit of the humble, and to revive the heart of the contrite ones."

God inhabits eternity. What an overwhelming thought! God is eternal; no beginning, no ending, God just was, is and will always be. Then He inhabits eternity in His holiness. God is Holy; perfect, without sin, complete in and of Himself. Now here's the thought: In light of who God is, how can we even begin to stand in His presence? The Lord tells us, with a contrite and humble spirit, but instead in arrogance and pride, we demand of this Holy One that He is in some way required to answer us, when in truth just to be able to stand in His presence is more honor than we deserve. Humility is the lesson for today.

Add your thoughts and/or prayer for the day

August 13
Isaiah 60-63

Isaiah 61:1-3
"(1) *The Spirit of the Lord GOD is upon me; because the LORD hath anointed me to preach good tidings unto the meek; he hath sent me to bind up the brokenhearted, to proclaim liberty to the captives, and the opening of the prison to them that are bound; (2) To proclaim the acceptable year of the LORD, and the day of vengeance of our God; to comfort all that mourn; (3) To appoint unto them that mourn in Zion, to give unto them beauty for ashes, the oil of joy for mourning, the garment of praise for the spirit of heaviness; that they might be called trees of righteousness, the planting of the LORD, that he might be glorified.*"

When we share with others the awesome grace, love and mercy of our Lord, we are giving that which is unlike anything else we can give them. It is through the knowledge of the Lord that they will find freedom, healing, beauty, joy, praise, and strength! Can anything be better than that? Keep sharing the Lord with others, the greatest gift of all.

Add your thoughts and/or prayer for the day

Isaiah 64:6
"But we are all as an unclean thing, and all our righteousnesses are as filthy rags; and we all do fade as a leaf; and our iniquities, like the wind, have taken us away."

Here Isaiah says that our very best is as filthy rags in the light of God's holiness. Yet the Lord told his disciples that they were to be holy, even as God our Father is holy. Truth is, that in us is no good thing. The righteousness we can produce falls way too short of what is demanded of God. Our only hope is that God will provide His righteousness for us and He did through Jesus Christ. Jesus, the sinless sacrifice for our sin offers us His holiness in exchange for our self-righteousness and sin. The undeserved favor of God providing us the righteousness required that we could not produce of ourselves. It is called grace, and it is received by faith.

Add your thoughts and/or prayer for the day

August 15
Jeremiah 1-3

Jeremiah 1:9-10
"(9) Then the LORD put forth his hand, and touched my mouth. And the LORD said unto me, Behold, I have put my words in thy mouth. (10) See, I have this day set thee over the nations and over the kingdoms, to root out, and to pull down, and to destroy, and to throw down, to build, and to plant."

The Lord, giving the prophet His word, describes what it is intended to accomplish. God's word is not just a devotional for us to spring off into our day with a song in our heart, it is the force that is designed to rule nations, pull down strongholds, destroy the strangle-hold of Satan, to establish us as believers ready for battle and to secure us so as to be unmovable in our faith. Don't take so lightly the reading and studying of God's word, it is your life's blood for living!

Add your thoughts and/or prayer for the day

August 16
Jeremiah 4-6

Jeremiah 5:12-13 ESV
*"(12) They have spoken falsely of the LORD and have said,
'He will do nothing; no disaster will come upon us, nor shall
we see sword or famine. (13) The prophets will become
wind; the word is not in them. Thus shall
it be done to them!'"*

Israel was to be judged because the preachers were not teaching the whole truth. They only spoke the things that people loved to hear, but refused to warn them of their sin and God's judgment. Today, it seems people swarm the churches that will preach a 'feel-good' message, but refuse to take a stand against sin and preach the hard truth of God's holiness and His judgment. Pray for preachers to be filled with the words of Christ and to have the boldness to stand for the truth!

Add your thoughts and/or prayer for the day

Jeremiah 7:18-19
"(18) The children gather wood, and the fathers kindle the fire, and the women knead their dough, to make cakes to the queen of heaven, and to pour out drink offerings unto other gods, that they may provoke me to anger. (19) Do they provoke me to anger? saith the LORD: do they not provoke themselves to the confusion of their own faces?"

God has given us clear direction to follow and to benefit from His leading, yet for the most part, we spend our days chasing our own cares. We teach our children to go after the worldly attractions, instead of teaching them the real joy of serving the Lord and others. Then, when those things don't produce what we had hoped, we come to the Lord and wonder what went wrong, confused at the outcome of our lives and the choices our children make. It is not hard to have the best that God has to offer, but you must be willing to do things God's way.

<u>**Add your thoughts and/or prayer for the day**</u>

August 18
Jeremiah 10-12

Jeremiah 10:10-11
"(10) But the LORD is the true God, he is the living God, and an everlasting king: at his wrath the earth shall tremble, and the nations shall not be able to abide his indignation. (11) Thus shall ye say unto them, The gods that have not made the heavens and the earth, even they shall perish from the earth, and from under these heavens."

The world seems to have forgotten that God the creator is the one who is in charge. They have replaced Him with all kinds of things and activities, but when God has had his fill of our disobedience, He can and will bring us back into to the reality that He is God and there is no other. It sure would be best if we began now to re-establish His Lordship, instead of waiting for His wrath to bring us there.

Add your thoughts and/or prayer for the day

August 19
Jeremiah 12-15

Jeremiah 14:22
"Are there any among the vanities of the Gentiles that can cause rain? or can the heavens give showers? art not thou he, O LORD our God? therefore we will wait upon thee: for thou hast made all these things."

In our attempt to hurry the things of God, we many times will jump into His affairs and use our own abilities to get what we think is God's will. Here we are reminded that there are things only God can bring to pass, like the rain. But the truth is, God has made all things, and not only in nature do we need to wait upon the Lord, but in every area of our lives. You will never be at fault for waiting upon the Lord, but you can get into a world of trouble when you run ahead of Him. Just wait, the rain will come in His time and it will be exactly what you need.

Add your thoughts and/or prayer for the day

August 20
Jeremiah 16-18

Jeremiah 18:3-4
"(3) Then I went down to the potter's house, and, behold, he wrought a work on the wheels. (4) And the vessel that he made of clay was marred in the hand of the potter: so he made it again another vessel, as seemed good to the potter to make it."

Just as the potter takes the clay and molds it to his liking and purpose, the Lord does the same with us as a nation and as individuals. If, in the process the clay becomes hard or has impurities in it, the potter will rework it until he gets what he wants. You understand that you are the clay that must stay moldable in the hands of the Master. It is His will that you must fulfill not your own. It is His design you must become in order to fulfill the purpose for which you were made. Until we yield to His will, we are just a lump of clay with no real purpose.

Add your thoughts and/or prayer for the day

Jeremiah 21:2
"Enquire, I pray thee, of the LORD for us; for
Nebuchadrezzar king of Babylon maketh war against us; if
so be that the LORD will deal with us according to all his
wondrous works, that he may go up from us."

King Zedekiah had sought to live by his own rules and have his own religion and is now in major trouble as he hears that the king of Babylon is coming to make war. In this dilemma, he turns quickly to the true man of God because he knows that he has connection with the one true God, the only one that could help. My, how people love living by their own rules and seeking out preachers who will tell them what they want to hear. But when trouble comes their way, they turn from their liberal preachers and go to those who hold the truth, wanting the Lord to pull them out of their self-willed problems. If only we would put ourselves under the authority of God's word and be obedient to it, then we wouldn't get ourselves into these problems.

Add your thoughts and/or prayer for the day

August 22
Jeremiah 22-24

Jeremiah 23:21-23
"(21) I have not sent these prophets, yet they ran: I have not spoken to them, yet they prophesied. (22) But if they had stood in my counsel, and had caused my people to hear my words, then they should have turned them from their evil way, and from the evil of their doings. (23) Am I a God at hand, saith the LORD, and not a God afar off?"

God was angry with the prophets that were saying all kinds of things, but were not sent by Him. There are today so many standing and saying they have a word from the Lord that are not from God. Their messages are not from God but from their own imaginations. God's word is where we get God's message. It is God's written word that provides for true repentance and changed lives. Be careful not to be drawn into the heresy of the false prophets of today. Know the Word, study the Word, live the Word.

Add your thoughts and/or prayer for the day

August 23
Jeremiah 25-27

Jeremiah 26:7-8
"(7) So the priests and the prophets and all the people heard Jeremiah speaking these words in the house of the LORD. (8) Now it came to pass, when Jeremiah had made an end of speaking all that the LORD had commanded him to speak unto all the people, that the priests and the prophets and all the people took him, saying, Thou shalt surely die."

Here again, we see the religious leaders and people turn on the prophet of God because he preaches the Word of the Lord. God was about to bring judgment on Judah and in His loving compassion He sends Jeremiah to warn them. He was to call them back to serving the Lord instead of the false gods they were serving. Not only do they refuse to return to serving God, they turn on the messenger that God had sent to warn them. They will be led into captivity because of their neglect to adhere to the Word of God. We might heed this message for ourselves. The Lord is calling us to repentance, what will be our response?

Add your thoughts and/or prayer for the day

August 24
Jeremiah 28-30

Jeremiah 29:11-13
"(11) For I know the thoughts that I think toward you, saith the LORD, thoughts of peace, and not of evil, to give you an expected end. (12) Then shall ye call upon me, and ye shall go and pray unto me, and I will hearken unto you. (13) And ye shall seek me, and find me, when ye shall search for me with all your heart."

We see and hear verse 11 quoted by many today, but this is a promise the Lord gave Judah so that during the seventy year bondage to Babylon, they would not lose heart. When we claim this verse for ourselves, it might be good to understand that God's timing is not our timing, and the 'expected end' might not come as we expect it. Better that we continue to seek the Lord with all our heart and search for Him in spite of our circumstances. Just remember our peace comes in Christ, not in our circumstances.

Add your thoughts and/or prayer for the day

Jeremiah 32:18-19
"(18) Thou shewest lovingkindness unto thousands, and recompensest the iniquity of the fathers into the bosom of their children after them: the Great, the Mighty God, the LORD of hosts, is his name, (19) Great in counsel, and mighty in work: for thine eyes are open upon all the ways of the sons of men: to give every one according to his ways, and according to the fruit of his doings:"

When you watch some people, you begin to wonder if they really have any concept of God. Just who He is? How awesome His power? How involved He is with every person? Do they realize that every breath they take is only theirs because the Lord loves them enough to give it? If they really understood this would they be doing the things they do or living the way they live? It seems obvious that they don't understand that the Lord will repay them according to the 'fruit of their doings".

<u>**Add your thoughts and/or prayer for the day**</u>

August 26
Jeremiah 34-36

Jeremiah 36:23-24
"(23) And it came to pass, that when Jehudi had read three or four leaves, he cut it with the penknife, and cast it into the fire that was on the hearth, until all the roll was consumed in the fire that was on the hearth. (24) Yet they were not afraid, nor rent their garments, neither the king, nor any of his servants that heard all these words."

Judah was in trouble and they had set a day to fast, but when the word of God was read, they did not know how to respond. When it was presented to the king, he burned it in complete disregard for it. The truth is that a person can try to change the word of God, refuse to study it, not believe it, even destroy it, but His Word will never bend to anyone's way of thinking. It is God's Word, it is true, it is eternal, and it is unchanging. It would be best that we believe and live by it and follow those who do the same.

Add your thoughts and/or prayer for the day

Jeremiah 39:15-16
"(15) Now the word of the LORD came unto Jeremiah, while he was shut up in the court of the prison, saying, (16) Go and speak to Ebedmelech the Ethiopian, saying, Thus saith the LORD of hosts, the God of Israel; Behold, I will bring my words upon this city for evil, and not for good; and they shall be accomplished in that day before thee."

God always keeps His word. He had warned Judah that He was going to bring judgment against them for their disobedience, but they continued with no regard to the Lord. God kept His word. When the Lord says, *'Be not deceived, God is not mocked, for whatsoever a man seweth, that shall he also reap'*, we can be sure that is exactly what will happen. If then, we want to receive God's best, we must plant seeds of obedience. Just as He will judge those who are disobedient to Him, He will reward those who obey. Which would you rather receive of the Lord? It really is your choice!

Add your thoughts and/or prayer for the day

August 28
Jeremiah 40-42

Jeremiah 42:5-6
"(5) Then they said to Jeremiah, The LORD be a true and faithful witness between us, if we do not even according to all things for the which the LORD thy God shall send thee to us. (6) Whether it be good, or whether it be evil, we will obey the voice of the LORD our God, to whom we send thee; that it may be well with us, when we obey the voice of the LORD our God."

The remnant of those who were left in Judah after the captivity of Babylon seem to be saying they wanted to make things right with the Lord in their request to Jeremiah. However, as you read further, you find that they really didn't mean it at all, but chose to do their own thing. So many times we are caught in our disobedience and will make a half-hearted attempt to satisfy God with our remorse. Because it is not sincere, we will soon resort back into our old ways. But when we get serious with the Lord, He will be serious with us. It would do us well to keep our promises to the Lord, because it is a sure thing that He will keep His with us.

Add your thoughts and/or prayer for the day

Jeremiah 44:16
"As for the word that thou hast spoken unto us in the name of the LORD, we will not hearken unto thee."

In the reading this morning, the remnant of Judah that God had permitted to remain in Canaan after the Babylonian captivity, had violated the word of the Lord to go into Egypt instead of remaining in Canaan. As the prophet brings them further warning of God's judgment because of their disobedience, this is their reply - how obstinate, how rebellious! We find that people who choose to live by their own rules will find any reason or excuse not to live by the rules of God's word. Amazingly, when they have buried themselves in sin and are receiving the consequences of their own decisions, they will cry out to God, as if in some way He had let them down. A person cannot live outside of God's word and expect to find any true joy or lasting fulfillment.

Add your thoughts and/or prayer for the day

Jeremiah 46:27
"But fear not thou, O my servant Jacob, and be not dismayed, O Israel: for, behold, I will save thee from afar off, and thy seed from the land of their captivity; and Jacob shall return, and be in rest and at ease, and none shall make him afraid."

"Jacob" refers to the nation of Israel, God's chosen people. Here is a promise to that nation that God will restore them after their captivity, and bring them to a time of real peace. This relates to the promise of the Lord's earthly kingdom He will establish for a thousand years at the close of Earth's history. Today, it is evident that Jacob is returning as they can't build housing fast enough for the amount of Israelites who are moving back into Israel. Although there is no peace for them at this time, their peace will come after the Lord's return. The signs of His return are eminent. So be ready, dear church, our redemption draweth nigh!

Add your thoughts and/or prayer for the day

Jeremiah 49:4-5
"(4) Wherefore gloriest thou in the valleys, thy flowing valley,
O backsliding daughter? that trusted in her treasures, saying,
Who shall come unto me? (5) Behold, I will bring a fear upon
thee, saith the Lord GOD of hosts, from all those that be about
thee; and ye shall be driven out every man right forth; and
none shall gather up him that wandereth."

The Lord, in His pronouncement of the judgment of the nations, confronts the Ammonites with their false security. This nation felt that it was outside of any kind of judgment because of its wealth and its economy, but God in verse 5 says they will not stand against His judgment. We Americans sometimes think we are above God's judgment because we have been so blessed. We have become complacent in our devotion to the One who made us a great nation, but we need to remember that God is still our Sovereign. It is only through His grace have we had such blessing.

<u>Add your thoughts and/or prayer for the day</u>

September 1
Lamentations 1-3

Lamentations 3:22-23
"(22) It is of the LORD'S mercies that we are not consumed, because his compassions fail not. (23) They are new every morning: great is thy faithfulness."

The writer is lamenting the loss of Jerusalem and the harsh punishment that has come at the hands of the Lord as a result of their sin, but then is reminded that if it weren't for the Lord's mercy they could have been consumed. Truth is that if we got what we deserved for our sinfulness we would have no hope at all, but God in His great love and compassion for us faithfully spares us from destruction. Every day we should remind ourselves of the Lord's great faithfulness to us. Like the song writer wrote, "Great is Thy faithfulness, O God my Father, There is no shadow of turning with Thee; Thou changest not, Thy compassions, they fail not as Thou hast been Thou forever wilt be."

Add your thoughts and/or prayer for the day

September 2
Lamentations 4-5

Lamentations 4:16
"The anger of the LORD hath divided them; he will no more regard them: they respected not the persons of the priests, they favoured not the elders."

Jeremiah gives us insight into part of the problem that brought about the Lord's judgment on the people of Israel. They had no use for the men of God nor for the elders. As the Lord sends out His called army of spokesmen who rightly divide the word of God, His intent is that His people listen and respond to their teaching and leadership. Just as important to the Lord is the respect and honor that we afford those who walk in wisdom from experience of age. Today, we find disrespect for both of these in our churches as well as our nation; it would be good to re-evaluate our values toward our elders, both spiritual and physical.

Add your thoughts and/or prayer for the day

September 3
Ezekiel 1-4

Ezekiel 3:27
"But when I speak with thee, I will open thy mouth, and thou shalt say unto them, Thus saith the Lord GOD; He that heareth, let him hear; and he that forbeareth, let him forbear: for they are a rebellious house."

Ezekiel is being called into the ministry of a prophet to preach of God's judgment upon a nation in rebellion to Him, a nation that would refuse to hear the message of God. If you sit under a man of God who honestly can preach "Thus saith the Lord God" because he has spent time with the Lord and His word and has a message from God, then listen with an attentive ear and an open heart refusing to rebel against God's word. And when you have heard the message of God and conviction falls upon your heart, run to the altars, seek repentance, and live as an example to those around you as a true follower of Jesus Christ.

Add your thoughts and/or prayer for the day

September 4
Ezekiel 5-8

Ezekiel 8:16
"And he brought me into the inner court of the LORD'S house, and, behold, at the door of the temple of the LORD, between the porch and the altar, were about five and twenty men, with their backs toward the temple of the LORD, and their faces toward the east; and they worshipped the sun toward the east."

The Lord is showing Ezekiel the sins of Judah and takes him to the temple to see men not worshipping God, but the sun. How wicked these men had become to blatantly stand at the Temple of God and worship something other than God! 1 Corinthians 3:16 says, "Know ye not that ye are the temple of God, and that the Spirit of God dwelleth in you?" So if we are the temple of God, how wicked are we to live lives that do not honour or bring witness to the fact that we have been bought with the price of the blood of our Lord and Savoir, Jesus Christ? Who do you worship? Would those around you each day agree that it is the Lord and Him alone that you serve?

Add your thoughts and/or prayer for the day

September 5
Ezekiel 9-12

Ezekiel 11:19-20
"(19) And I will give them one heart, and I will put a new spirit within you; and I will take the stony heart out of their flesh, and will give them an heart of flesh: (20) That they may walk in my statutes, and keep mine ordinances, and do them: and they shall be my people, and I will be their God."

A promise to Israel was that the Lord will gather His people and will give them one heart, a new spirit and a desire to live in obedience to Him. This is exactly what the Lord does for those who put their trust in Him. He makes us part of His family. He gives us the indwelling Holy Spirit. Through Him we are able to live in obedience to Him and He is our God and no other. What an awesome promise! What an awesome God we serve!

Add your thoughts and/or prayer for the day

September 6
Ezekiel 13-16

Ezekiel 14:13-14
"(13) Son of man, when the land sinneth against me by trespassing grievously, then will I stretch out mine hand upon it, and will break the staff of the bread thereof, and will send famine upon it, and will cut off man and beast from it: (14) Though these three men, Noah, Daniel, and Job, were in it, they should deliver but their own souls by their righteousness, saith the Lord GOD."

When the judgment of God falls there are those who think they can ride upon the spiritual coat tails of others, but the Lord makes it very clear in this passage no one escapes judgment by the deeds of others. Every person will have to stand upon their own decisions. Needless to say, unless you have received the righteousness of Jesus Christ offered by His love and grace, there is no escape from God's final judgment.

Add your thoughts and/or prayer for the day

September 7
Ezekiel 17-20

Ezekiel 20:19-20
"(19) I am the LORD your God; walk in my statutes, and keep my judgments, and do them; (20) And hallow my sabbaths; and they shall be a sign between me and you, that ye may know that I am the LORD your God."

How can we be obedient to the statutes and judgments of the Lord if we do not know them? So many are failing in their walk with God simply because they will not read, study and apply God's word to their lives. How frustrating it must be to the Lord to have given us such detailed instruction only to have us neglect it for all the reasons we give. It is through the application of His word that we identify ourselves as children of His. It is through the simple act of setting aside time for serving Him that declares to the world that we belong to Him.

Add your thoughts and/or prayer for the day

Ezekiel 22:29-30
"(29) The people of the land have used oppression, and exercised robbery, and have vexed the poor and needy: yea, they have oppressed the stranger wrongfully. (30) And I sought for a man among them, that should make up the hedge, and stand in the gap before me for the land, that I should not destroy it: but I found none."

The Lord, in looking at His people, a nation set apart to bring Him witness to rest of the world, can find no one of honor or integrity to keep Him from bringing judgment against them. All God wants is someone that will stand up, to be a man or woman of God. He is looking for a person of integrity that would carry His cause, His witness, His word to a lost and dying world. You have the opportunity to be the one standing in the gap for those around you; will you be that man or woman in your world today?

Add your thoughts and/or prayer for the day

September 9
Ezekiel 25-28

Ezekiel 28:26
"And they (Israel) shall dwell safely therein, and shall build houses, and plant vineyards; yea, they shall dwell with confidence, when I have executed judgments upon all those that despise them round about them; and they shall know that I am the LORD their God."

Much of what we will read in the book of Ezekiel will be prophecies of the end times. Here is one of those passages that speak of God's love for the nation Israel and how He promises peace to them and will give them their land to live in. We are living in a time when there is great turmoil in Israel. The nations around them are always threatening them and trying to do them harm, but there is coming a day and it may be soon, when God will intervene and judge those nations who oppose her. Dear church, our time draws short; let us be found faithful in these last days.

Add your thoughts and/or prayer for the day

Ezekiel 30:12
"And I will make the rivers dry, and sell the land into the hand of the wicked: and I will make the land waste, and all that is therein, by the hand of strangers: I the LORD have spoken it."

God's sovereignty is one of His greatest attributes. This is His authority and control over everything. Nations He has allowed to rise to power for the purpose of dealing with Israel; He will bring to destruction for their denial to recognize Him as sovereign Lord. Nothing escapes His attention, every detail is covered by Him and He will judge sin. But this sovereign authority can also offer grace to whomever and whenever He chooses, because He is sovereign. Who are we to question His divine order? Instead we should be honored to call Him our Lord, our Savior, our Father.

Add your thoughts and/or prayer for the day

September 11
Ezekiel 33-36

Ezekiel 34:23-24
"(23) And I will set up one shepherd over them, and he shall feed them, even my servant David; he shall feed them, and he shall be their shepherd. (24) And I the LORD will be their God, and my servant David a prince among them; I the LORD have spoken it."

The Lord Jesus will return physically and establish His kingdom on earth for a thousand years. During that time this passage speaks of *'my servant David'* being the chief shepherd. This is in reference to Jesus who will be the final King to sit upon the throne of David. With the chaos that exists all over the world today it almost seems impossible but we can trust the Word of God that the day of Christ's return will come in power and glory! The earth will be restored to its pre-fall status and peace will be worldwide. As we look forward to His reign on Earth, that same power and glory and peace can be experienced today in our lives as we allow Him to sit upon the throne of our hearts.

Add your thoughts and/or prayer for the day

Ezekiel 39:7
"So will I make my holy name known in the midst of my people Israel; and I will not let them pollute my holy name any more: and the heathen shall know that I am the LORD, the Holy One in Israel."

How awesome this will be when the Lord is finally recognized by all that He is the LORD. Won't that be an awesome thing to see and be a part of, to not have to defend ourselves for our beliefs, because everyone will know that He is the Holy One in Israel? In our lives we may not have been able to always be on the winning side of things, but one thing is for sure, if you have chosen to follow Christ you're on the one team that really matters in the end. In the end, the Lord is the victor, King of kings and Lord of lords, and we are all winners in Him!

<u>Add your thoughts and/or prayer for the day</u>

September 13
Ezekiel 41-44

Ezekiel 43:4-5
"(4) And the glory of the LORD came into the house by the way of the gate whose prospect is toward the east. (5) So the spirit took me up, and brought me into the inner court; and, behold, the glory of the LORD filled the house."

In our reading we have seen the new millennial temple described in detail. It will be holy in every aspect and at its completion the Lord will come in all of His glory and fill the temple with His presence in the sight of everyone. This will be His throne during His millennial reign. It is going to be glorious! Just as the Lord will enter that temple, know for certain that as we have invited Him into our lives, He has possessed our lives as His temple. Even as the future temple will be holy, His desire is that our lives be holy as well as it is the place of His dwelling.

Add your thoughts and/or prayer for the day

September 14
Ezekiel 45-48

Ezekiel 46:13
"Thou shalt daily prepare a burnt offering unto the LORD of a lamb of the first year without blemish: thou shalt prepare it every morning."

During the millennial reign of Christ, there will be daily offerings made every morning, not for the atonement for sin, but for a reminder of the atonement that was made through Christ the perfect Lamb of God. We too, should consider a daily offering of ourselves as a constant reminder of who it was that bought us with a price, atoned for our sin, and should victoriously reign in our lives. This devotional time should begin every day and then consume us as we go throughout the day. When we get too busy to spend the first part of our day with the Lord, then we have become way too busy!

Add your thoughts and/or prayer for the day

September 15
Daniel 1-4

Daniel 3:17-18
"(17) If it be so, our God whom we serve is able to deliver us from the burning fiery furnace, and he will deliver us out of thine hand, O king. (18) But if not, be it known unto thee, O king, that we will not serve thy gods, nor worship the golden image which thou hast set up."

This is the answer given when these men of true godly integrity were told to bow to the image the king had set up. Oh how this world needs men and women with a backbone and a commitment to the Lord that surpasses the temptations of this world. Would it be that when the children of God are asked to violate what they know is right, that they would stand by faith and allow God to be honored in their lives. Be a man or woman of godly character and stand for what is right and trust God for the outcome.

Add your thoughts and/or prayer for the day

September 16
Daniel 5-8

Daniel 8:25
"And through his policy also he shall cause craft to prosper in his hand; and he shall magnify himself in his heart, and by peace shall destroy many: he shall also stand up against the Prince of princes; but he shall be broken without hand."

Daniel has two visions of the end times, in this one he witnesses the power and destruction that the antichrist will bring upon the earth and even stand against the Lord Himself. But against the Lord it says he will be broken without hand. Satan's all out attacks although damaging cannot even touch the power of our Lord. We are told that the Lord will send an angel to bind Satan during the millennium. The Lord won't even dirty His hands in defeating our enemy. We are to be aware of Satan's devices, but remember, greater is He that is in you than he that is in the world.

Add your thoughts and/or prayer for the day

Daniel 10:19

"And said, O man greatly beloved, fear not: peace be unto thee, be strong, yea, be strong. And when he had spoken unto me, I was strengthened, and said, Let my lord speak; for thou hast strengthened me."

Daniel receives and shares the great prophesy of the end times, but as the Lord appears to him, his strength is gone. It is as the Lord speaks to him that he receives the strength to follow through with what the Lord has given him to do. God will not put upon us anything that He has not prepared us to do and part of that preparation is to empower us for the task. Never fear the work God has given you to do because of your weakness but instead find your strength in His word.

Add your thoughts and/or prayer for the day

September 18
Hosea 1-5

Hosea 4:6
"My people are destroyed for lack of knowledge: because thou hast rejected knowledge, I will also reject thee, that thou shalt be no priest to me: seeing thou hast forgotten the law of thy God, I will also forget thy children."

In days past, we taught our children the Bible, its stories, and about Jesus. However, it seems as of late that even with all the new technology that allows us to have a more ready access to the Word of God that we do not spend time reading and studying it for ourselves much less teaching it to our children. The Lord warns his people that because they had rejected His law that He would forget their children. It is time we reclaimed our right and responsibility as parents and guardians and make sure that our children have been taught the truths of God's word.

Add your thoughts and/or prayer for the day

Hosea 6:6
"For I desired mercy, and not sacrifice; and the knowledge of God more than burnt offerings."

We hear it over and over from God's own word that in our worship of Him He is not concerned about what we do, but what we know because what we know will determine what we do. So many will live out their spiritual lives seeking to satisfy their worship by doing or giving anything and everything except the one thing that really honors the Lord - knowing Him. How can we know Him, if we never seek to learn of Him through the words He has sent to us? Don't be satisfied with just what others say of God's word. Read God's love letter to you for yourself!

Add your thoughts and/or prayer for the day

September 20
Hosea 11-14

Hosea 14:9 ESV
"Whoever is wise, let him understand these things; whoever is discerning, let him know them; for the ways of the LORD are right, and the upright walk in them, but transgressors stumble in them."

How true this is when it comes to the truth of God's word. There are those who honestly desire the things of the Lord and for them the Word of God is powerful, full of wisdom and instruction, a place to find the answers for life's situations. However, to those who are hell bent on living after their own wisdom, their own selfish driven desires, the Word of God is only a book that causes them to stumble, a place to argue against the Lord. We shouldn't be so surprised by the world's reaction to our stand on biblical issues, they just don't get it.

Add your thoughts and/or prayer for the day

September 21
Joel 1-3

Joel 2:1-2
"(1) Blow ye the trumpet in Zion, and sound an alarm in my holy mountain: let all the inhabitants of the land tremble: for the day of the LORD cometh, for it is nigh at hand; A day of darkness and of gloominess, a day of clouds and of thick darkness, as the morning spread upon the mountains: a great people and a strong; there hath not been ever the like, neither shall be any more after it, even to the years of many generations."

Joel's prophesies concern Israel and the second coming of Christ at the close of the great tribulation. Here he warns of the impending coming of the Lord that is in our day still to come. We need to understand that as urgent as the warning was then, it certainly should be a warning for us today some twenty-five hundred years later. You can be sure that Jesus is coming soon and we need to stand ready at all times!

Add your thoughts and/or prayer for the day

September 22
Amos 1-3

Amos 2:11-12
"(11) And I raised up of your sons for prophets, and of your young men for Nazarites. Is it not even thus, O ye children of Israel? saith the LORD. (12) But ye gave the Nazarites wine to drink; and commanded the prophets, saying, Prophesy not."

God had given Israel men of God, but their response to these men of God was to force them to violate their integrity and not to preach. People who feel they are doing right in their own eyes, do not want to hear what the word of God says, but instead will do everything in their power to pull that man or woman of God down to their level. Learn to stand alone if you must, but never violate your integrity nor your spiritual calling to satisfy someone other than the Lord.

Add your thoughts and/or prayer for the day

September 23
Amos 4-6

Amos 4:13
"For, lo, he that formeth the mountains, and createth the wind, and declareth unto man what is his thought, that maketh the morning darkness, and treadeth upon the high places of the earth, The LORD, The God of hosts, is his name."

In this passage of scripture, the Lord reminds Israel of all that He has done to call them back to him, but they have refused. Now He reminds them of who He is. What a shame that the creator and sustainer of life itself has to remind His creation that He is God. Our biggest problem is that we want to be god, the god of our lives, but there can only be one God. Be reminded today of who is God of your life. He has definitely earned the position and will do a much better job of it than you.

Add your thoughts and/or prayer for the day

September 24
Amos 7-9

Amos 8:11-12
"(11) Behold, the days come, saith the Lord GOD, that I will send a famine in the land, not a famine of bread, nor a thirst for water, but of hearing the words of the LORD: (12) And they shall wander from sea to sea, and from the north even to the east, they shall run to and fro to seek the word of the LORD, and shall not find it."

According to this prophecy, as the end times approach, preachers will turn from preaching the truth of God's word to heralding a humanistic gospel wanting to satisfy rather than call to repentance. Today, we see preachers bent on building bigger empires have sold out to preaching around the word of God. They are so afraid of offending someone that they refuse be honest with God's word and preach 'thus saith the Lord'. The church has been weakened to the point that now even the governments have turned to using their powers to shut the mouths of preachers who will preach and stand for the Truth. The famine that Amos is referring has begun.

<u>Add your thoughts and/or prayer for the day</u>

September 25
Obadiah 1

Obadiah 1:3-4
"(3) The pride of thine heart hath deceived thee, thou that dwellest in the clefts of the rock, whose habitation is high; that saith in his heart, Who shall bring me down to the ground? (4) Though thou exalt thyself as the eagle, and though thou set thy nest among the stars, thence will I bring thee down, saith the LORD."

Obadiah's prophesy had to do with the Northern kingdom, Israel, and their aristocratic arrogance. They thought they had no need for God because they had provided for their own security. Much like the nations and people of our world are moving in areas of self sufficiency never realizing the involvement of the Lord in all their scheming and planning. God is God, sovereign above all others! When He declares it is His time, nothing will stop Him. Serve Him today.

Add your thoughts and/or prayer for the day

Jonah 2:8
"Those who pay regard to vain idols forsake their hope of steadfast love."

What a simple statement, but what a profound truth! This mass of humanity we call our world for the most part will spend their lives looking for real love and real relationship in all the wrong places with all the wrong people. They pay homage to jobs, money, recreation, with things they can own or things they can do, with little if any regard to the one person who can give them more peace, more joy, more love than anyone or anything. They will question their existence in time only to find their lives lack real substance or purpose except for the things they have acquired and yet in all they have and all they have done they will have not have satisfied their thirst for real love and acceptance. If you are spending your time paying regard to the vain idols of this world, you are missing the steadfast love of the God who created you, loves you and wants you.

Add your thoughts and/or prayer for the day

September 27
Micah 1-3

Micah 4:2
"And many nations shall come, and say, Come, and let us go up to the mountain of the LORD, and to the house of the God of Jacob; and he will teach us of his ways, and we will walk in his paths: for the law shall go forth of Zion, and the word of the LORD from Jerusalem."

Micah gives us a picture of the end times when the Lord Himself shall reign from Jerusalem described here as the mountain of the Lord. What a wonderful day that will be when the whole world will seek His teaching and have a desire to walk in His godly footsteps. Hang on dear saints of God, the persecution that we will endure shall only last for a season. His time will come and we will see and be a part of His victory. As Paul told us, stand fast, unmovable, always abounding in the work of the Lord for you know that your labor is not in vain in the Lord.

Add your thoughts and/or prayer for the day

Micah 7:7-8
"(7) Therefore I will look unto the LORD; I will wait for the God of my salvation: my God will hear me. (8) Rejoice not against me, O mine enemy: when I fall, I shall arise; when I sit in darkness, the LORD shall be a light unto me."

Dear saint of God, keep your eyes upon the Master especially in times of trouble, heart-ache, and suffering for He hears your prayers and feels your heart need. Don't allow the enemy to win in these matters for it is in these things we can find the Master's strength. Even if you fall, know that the Lord will raise you up again and in those dark times of your life let the enemy know you will find your light in the Lord. Just be patient. Waiting is key to experiencing God's presence.

Add your thoughts and/or prayer for the day

Nahum 1:6-7
"(6) Who can stand before his indignation? and who can abide in the fierceness of his anger? his fury is poured out like fire, and the rocks are thrown down by him. (7) The LORD is good, a strong hold in the day of trouble; and he knoweth them that trust in him."

Nahum pronouncing judgment against a wicked city gives insight to the truth of God's attributes. The Lord can and will judge evil yet in His faithfulness he will protect and love those who put their trust in Him. Many will not want to hear God's message of judgment, but God is a just God. Yes, God is a loving, merciful God but He is also one who will sit as the righteous judge demanding holiness. Even if you are one of his children he has said He chastens those He loves. Walk in His holiness and trust Him for your strength.

Add your thoughts and/or prayer for the day

September 30
Habakkuk 1-3

Habakkuk 1:12
"Art thou not from everlasting, O LORD my God, mine Holy One? we shall not die. O LORD, thou hast ordained them for judgment; and, O mighty God, thou hast established them for correction."

Habakkuk, in the previous verses had asked the question we hear from so many, 'Why is there so much evil in the world?' The Lord did not create man to just live and then cease to exist, as some would believe. The soul of man will live forever, and it was God's original design for man to live in perfect relationship with Him. However, man chose to follow his own sinful desire over the desire of the Lord and as a result was put under the judgment of God. The answer to the question, "why so much evil in the world?" is simply that man chose to make himself god instead of the Lord being God. The holiness of God requires Him to *"ordain them for judgment"* and correction upon all that live in sin. So, the next time you are tempted to ask why the world has become so wicked, remember it is our choice to disobey God that caused it.

Add your thoughts and/or prayer for the day

October 1
Zephaniah 1-3

Zephaniah 3:17
"The LORD thy God in the midst of thee is mighty; he will save, he will rejoice over thee with joy; he will rest in his love, he will joy over thee with singing."

Zephaniah's prophecy is one of the devastation that will be brought during the great tribulation referred to as the day of the Lord. Almost hidden in its verses we find this one verse of promise to the remnant people of God. No matter what you may be going through, how tough the situation, God has a promise for those who put their trust in Him. He is mighty to save; His joy for you will be demonstrated in His love for you. Find the truth of His love in the midst of the lies of your situation. God is love and He loves you with all His heart!

Add your thoughts and/or prayer for the day

October 2
Haggai 1-2

Haggai 1:4-6
"(4) Is it a time for you yourselves to dwell in your paneled houses, while this house lies in ruins? (5) Now, therefore, thus says the LORD of hosts: Consider your ways. (6) You have sown much, and harvested little. You eat, but you never have enough; you drink, but you never have your fill. You clothe yourselves, but no one is warm. And he who earns wages does so to put them into a bag with holes."

The people were putting their own selfish desires before the service of the Lord and because of that they were suffering. Doesn't it make you wonder what our nation would look like if the Lord were considered first instead of last? If God were first place we would not be suffering from all the ills that we have brought upon ourselves. Even in our own lives, as long as we put our needs and wants above the service and worship of our Lord we can expect to see little come of our efforts. Put God first!

Add your thoughts and/or prayer for the day

October 3
Zechariah 1-4

Zechariah 1:3-4
"(3) Therefore say thou unto them, Thus saith the LORD of hosts; Turn ye unto me, saith the LORD of hosts, and I will turn unto you, saith the LORD of hosts. (4) Be ye not as your fathers, unto whom the former prophets have cried, saying, Thus saith the LORD of hosts; Turn ye now from your evil ways, and from your evil doings: but they did not hear, nor hearken unto me, saith the LORD."

Just because others haven't listened or responded to the call of God does not mean we can't. The truth is and always has been that if we will turn to the Lord He is always ready to receive us. If there has ever been a time when the people of God need to repent and seek after the Lord, it is now. What has become comfortable to you that used to be a sin you would never consider? Turn to Him and He promises to turn to you.

Add your thoughts and/or prayer for the day

Zechariah 6:12-13
"(12) *And speak unto him, saying, Thus speaketh the LORD of hosts, saying, Behold the man whose name is The BRANCH; and he shall grow up out of his place, and he shall build the temple of the LORD: (13) Even he shall build the temple of the LORD; and he shall bear the glory, and shall sit and rule upon his throne; and he shall be a priest upon his throne: and the counsel of peace shall be between them both."*

How awesome to think that this Old Testament prophet under the divine inspiration of the Holy Spirit writes about something that will take place over two millennia from his time on earth. This 'Branch' is none other than Jesus Christ. At His first coming He grew up out of his place. When He will come at His second coming He will establish His rule from the new temple here on earth. Just as sure as Jesus came the first time He will return again and it won't be long. Be ready dear child of God, the Lord is coming soon.

Add your thoughts and/or prayer for the day

Zechariah 11:11
*"And it was broken in that day: and so the poor of the flock
that waited upon me knew that it was the word of the LORD."*

This remnant of God's chosen called "the poor of the flock" could look at what others would see as a broken covenant and just trust the Lord through it all. The reason this was so, was because they knew it was the word of the Lord! People who spend little or no time reading and studying the Bible will struggle with the plans of God. Their faith is only in what they understand or perceive to be true, but God's word gives a much clearer picture of our God and His sovereignty. The more time you spend coming to know the word of the Lord, the more you become aware of the Lord of the word. Don't just study and read the parts that are easy to understand and digest; get into the parts that come with much time and study. Just remember the more you have to dig and work at it, the greater the find!

Add your thoughts and/or prayer for the day

October 6
Zechariah 12-14

Zechariah 12:10
"And I will pour upon the house of David, and upon the inhabitants of Jerusalem, the spirit of grace and of supplications: and they shall look upon me whom they have pierced, and they shall mourn for him, as one mourneth for his only son, and shall be in bitterness for him, as one that is in bitterness for his firstborn."

As Christians, we can look with great anticipation to the coming of the Lord and a time upon earth when all men will worship the Lord and him alone. In that time, they will see His scars as a daily reminder of what He did to pay the price for their sin. They will acknowledge the fact of their need for salvation instead of defending their sin and rejecting Christ's offer of forgiveness and regeneration. However, as we wait for His coming, we must continue to point people to the Savior and pray they find that amazing grace.

Add your thoughts and/or prayer for the day

October 7
Malachi 1-4

Malachi 1:13
"Ye said also, Behold, what a weariness is it! and ye have snuffed at it, saith the LORD of hosts; and ye brought that which was torn, and the lame, and the sick; thus ye brought an offering: should I accept this of your hand? saith the LORD."

If the Lord saw the disgust of people toward His worship in Malachi's day, you have to wonder what He sees today. Today people find every reason in the world not to serve or worship the Lord and then if they do, their offering is whatever they have left over. It is only if they have time or if they have anything left, or to present their hand-me-downs as an afterthought offering for the Lord. What is even stranger than their offerings is their expectation for some kind of recognition for their sacrifice. If you are going to serve the Lord give Him your best in everything you do or give!

Add your thoughts and/or prayer for the day

Matthew 2:5-6
"(5) And [the priests and scribes] said unto [Herod], In Bethlehem of Judaea: for thus it is written by the prophet, (6) And thou Bethlehem, in the land of Juda, art not the least among the princes of Juda: for out of thee shall come a Governor, that shall rule my people Israel."

The priests and scribes knew the scriptures well enough to tell Herod where their Messiah was to be born, yet didn't care enough to check out the wise men's claim of Jesus being born. What a lack of genuineness on their part as the holy men and spiritual leaders of that day! Oh, but how much more ingenuous are those of us today who proclaim the name of Christ as our Savior but have little time or put forth any or little effort to serve and worship the One who loves us so. Don't be satisfied with just the knowledge of the Savior; give your life to serve Him, worship Him, and live for Him.

Add your thoughts and/or prayer for the day

Matthew 6:12
"And forgive us our debts, as we forgive our debtors."

Jesus taught often on the need for forgiveness and its importance to the continued relationship with Him. So we must consider that forgiveness is key to the Christian's walk. We receive it so freely from our Lord, and yet it does not flow so freely from us to others. We must come to understand that forgiveness is the benefactor to more peace, more love, more acceptance, more freedom. You will find that forgiveness benefits the giver so much more than the recipient. So go ahead and forgive. It is a God thing to do and His peace is waiting on you!

Add your thoughts and/or prayer for the day

October 10
Matthew 7-9

Matthew 7:21-23
"(21) Not every one that saith unto me, Lord, Lord, shall enter into the kingdom of heaven; but he that doeth the will of my Father which is in heaven. (22) Many will say to me in that day, Lord, Lord, have we not prophesied in thy name? and in thy name have cast out devils? and in thy name done many wonderful works? (23) And then will I profess unto them, I never knew you: depart from me, ye that work iniquity."

Just belonging to a church, or having some experience which seems godly, does not assure you of eternal life. It is clear in this passage there are many who seem to be doing some great religious things, but the Lord says He does not know them. Be sure you are tied to the truth, the real Truth, Jesus Christ. Your eternal life depends upon it!

Add your thoughts and/or prayer for the day

October 11
Matthew 10-12

Matthew 11:28-30
"(28) Come unto me, all ye that labour and are heavy laden, and I will give you rest. (29) Take my yoke upon you, and learn of me; for I am meek and lowly in heart: and ye shall find rest unto your souls. (30) For my yoke is easy, and my burden is light."

Not sure why, but as humans trying to live as Christians we turn it into work and labor hard at it. The Lord calls us to His work that He says is easy and light. Consider He has called you to put His 'yoke' on yourself. The yoke was designed for two oxen to share in the load. Jesus is calling us to stop trying to do it ourselves and come in partnership with Him. When you are yoked up with the Lord you will find He really carries the weight of the load making it easy while the yoke itself is light.

Add your thoughts and/or prayer for the day

October 12
Matthew 13-15

Matthew 14:29-30
"(29) And he said, Come. And when Peter was come down out of the ship, he walked on the water, to go to Jesus. (30) But when he saw the wind boisterous, he was afraid; and beginning to sink, he cried, saying, Lord, save me."

How many times has the Lord called us out to walk by faith, not concerning ourselves with the circumstances that we see, but to keep our eyes fixed on Him. It is through this kind of faith that He is pleased. But we, like Peter, will let the stuff of earth rob us of the victory the Lord would allow and we begin to sink in our own mess. Don't let outside influences rob you of the joy of walking with your Savior, keep your eyes on Jesus and your faith in Him!

Add your thoughts and/or prayer for the day

October 13
Matthew 16-18

Matthew 16:23-24
"(23) But he turned, and said unto Peter, Get thee behind me, Satan: thou art an offence unto me: for thou savourest not the things that be of God, but those that be of men. (24) Then said Jesus unto his disciples, If any man will come after me, let him deny himself, and take up his cross, and follow me."

What offended the Lord? Peter had loved the things of men more than the things of God. Oh how He must be offended with most of what we do as our concentration is on our own pleasures and own stuff instead of upon those eternal things of God. No wonder the Lord tells us to take up our cross and follow Him. The cross was an executioner's tool for putting to death the offender. We should continually be putting those things that offend the Lord on our cross and getting them out of our lives.

Add your thoughts and/or prayer for the day

October 14
Matthew 19-21

Matthew 19:25-26
"(25) When his disciples heard it, they were exceedingly amazed, saying, Who then can be saved? (26) But Jesus beheld them, and said unto them, With men this is impossible; but with God all things are possible."

Jesus had just showed how that it was impossible for a man to be good enough to earn eternal life. He said it would be easier for a camel to pass through the eye of a needle. But what is impossible for man is possible with God. Your salvation cannot be earned or deserved by something you think you can do, it only comes through the righteousness that God has provided for you through Jesus Christ. So what is impossible for you, God does for you!

Add your thoughts and/or prayer for the day

Matthew 24:4-5
"(4) And Jesus answered and said unto them, Take heed that no man deceive you. (5) For many shall come in my name, saying, I am Christ; and shall deceive many."

One of the signs of the return of Christ is that of the deceivers. Men and women who will rise to preach another gospel, a gospel that will draw people away from the true gospel of Jesus' death, burial and resurrection. Be careful, in this passage Jesus goes on to say that these 'false prophets shall show great signs and wonders; insomuch that, if it were possible, they shall deceive the very elect.' You better know what you believe and why you believe it. Don't get sucked up into religious hype, stay grounded in the truth of the gospel.

Add your thoughts and/or prayer for the day

October 16
Matthew 25-28

Matthew 26:74-75
"(74) Then began he to curse and to swear, saying, I know not the man. And immediately the cock crew. (75) And Peter remembered the word of Jesus, which said unto him, Before the cock crow, thou shalt deny me thrice. And he went out, and wept bitterly."

Peter's denial of the Lord is one of those stories that as we read it, we must wonder how often we have been caught in circumstances that we could have stood for the Lord but for some reason we didn't. We, like Peter, will say we would never deny the Lord, but in truth we deny Him every day when we call ourselves Christian, yet our lives fall way short of being Christ-like. To avoid denying our Lord, it will require a complete dependence upon Him for our strength, for without Him we can do nothing.

Add your thoughts and/or prayer for the day

October 17
Mark 1-3

Mark 1:35-37
"(35) And in the morning, rising up a great while before day, he went out, and departed into a solitary place, and there prayed. (36) And Simon and they that were with him followed after him. (37) And when they had found him, they said unto him, All men seek for thee."

Jesus, the one who created the universe, had power to heal the sick and forgive sin and still knew that in all that He did, He needed to stay connected to the Father. While in the midst of ministering to so many and many seeking Him out with needs, Jesus knew what was most important and that was to spend time alone with God the Father. Never underestimate the importance of prayer. If Jesus needed to be alone with the Father, how much more do we need that quiet time? Never get to thinking you're so important and your work so necessary that you don't keep a priority on your quiet time with your Father.

Add your thoughts and/or prayer for the day

October 18
Mark 4-6

Mark 6:11
"And whosoever shall not receive you, nor hear you, when ye depart thence, shake off the dust under your feet for a testimony against them. Verily I say unto you, It shall be more tolerable for Sodom and Gomorrha in the day of judgment, than for that city."

Jesus is sending out the disciples to preach and this is His instruction. The Lord makes His truth known to all, but there are those who will refuse to listen, to heed, and to repent and to them their destruction is upon their own heads. It is our responsibility to herald the truth of the gospel; it is man's responsibility to respond and the Lord's responsibility to save. Be faithful, no matter the response, to love others enough to tell them of the Lord's offer of grace.

Add your thoughts and/or prayer for the day

Mark 8:34
"And when he had called the people unto him with his disciples also, he said unto them, Whosoever will come after me, let him deny himself, and take up his cross, and follow me."

Jesus says this to his disciples before He has gone to the cross, so try to understand it from their perspective. What they heard was that to follow the Lord they would need to deny themselves and should be prepared to die. This was truly a call to total commitment. Today people serve God out of convenience, but the Lord calls us to commitment; total, 100%, sold out, ready to die for Him commitment in order to follow Him. Being a follower of Jesus is not for the squeamish or half hearted! So what about you? Are you all in?

Add your thoughts and/or prayer for the day

October 20
Mark 10-12

Mark 12:43-44
"(43) And he called unto him his disciples, and saith unto them, Verily I say unto you, That this poor widow hath cast more in, than all they which have cast into the treasury: (44) For all they did cast in of their abundance; but she of her want did cast in all that she had, even all her living."

Oh how the Lord wants us to demonstrate our love and faith in the area of giving. This story shows that it is not the amount of the offering, but the amount of sacrifice that demonstrates our love for Him. Some only give out of their abundance the leftovers, when as children of grace we should give of the first, the best, before we do anything else. Just remember it is not our money that God wants, it's our hearts.

Add your thoughts and/or prayer for the day

October 21
Mark 13-16

Mark 13:35-37
"(35) *Watch ye therefore: for ye know not when the master of the house cometh, at even, or at midnight, or at the cockcrowing, or in the morning: (36) Lest coming suddenly he find you sleeping. (37) And what I say unto you I say unto all, Watch."*

How exciting to live in this time as we do! As imminent as the Lord spoke of His return to the disciples two thousand years ago, think how close we must be to seeing Him come for His own. The church must remain vigilant as ever to stand ready and diligent at His work, the only work that will last. However, some have already grown cold and even oblivious to the nearness of the hour as they have become consumed with worldly activities that keep them from the work of God. The Lord said to watch, be on guard, be ready! Don't stop now, dear saint of God, the Lord is coming!

Add your thoughts and/or prayer for the day

October 22
Luke 1-3

Luke 2:11-12
"(11) For unto you is born this day in the city of David a Saviour, which is Christ the Lord. (12) And this shall be a sign unto you; Ye shall find the babe wrapped in swaddling clothes, lying in a manger."

On occasion we have given witness to the birth of royalty in England, with all of their pomp and ceremony. When royalty is born, one would never expect it come in an animal's stable or the use of a food trough for a basinet, but that is exactly what happened when the King of kings was born. To the shepherds the welcomed news of the Shepherd King born in such a way was the introduction to the ministry of Jesus as the Servant King. He was of men, approachable, accessible and available just as He is today! If you have not yet met this Savior, why not come and meet your King today? His name is JESUS!

Add your thoughts and/or prayer for the day

Luke 6:38
"Give, and it shall be given unto you; good measure, pressed down, and shaken together, and running over, shall men give into your bosom. For with the same measure that ye mete withal it shall be measured to you again."

One can never out give God! No matter how or what you give, the promise of scripture is that God will return it with interest. The problem does not lie with what God will do, because God always keeps His word. The problem lies with us and what we will do based upon our faith in God and whether we really believe that God will keep his word. We put so much faith in what we can do, but so little faith in what God will do and it is proven in the way we give. Do you trust God? Do you love Him? If it is true, then it will be witnessed in the way you give.

Add your thoughts and/or prayer for the day

Luke 9:48
"And said unto them, Whosoever shall receive this child in my name receiveth me: and whosoever shall receive me receiveth him that sent me: for he that is least among you all, the same shall be great."

It is clear from the word of God that we demonstrate our love for the Lord by the way we treat others. This makes sense when the Lord is asked of the greatest commandment and ties our deep love for the Lord with our love for others. We live in a busy world that does things in fractions of seconds, but to care for others takes time that we think we don't have and resources that seem little enough just for our own. The Lord is clear that as His servants we will find the time and the resources required to demonstrate His love to others.

Add your thoughts and/or prayer for the day

Luke 10:40-42
"(40) But Martha was cumbered about much serving, and came to him, and said, Lord, dost thou not care that my sister hath left me to serve alone? bid her therefore that she help me. (41) And Jesus answered and said unto her, Martha, Martha, thou art careful and troubled about many things: (42) But one thing is needful: and Mary hath chosen that good part, which shall not be taken away from her."

Martha was a hard worker and loved to serve others. The problem came when she began to see that her sister did not help her because she chose to sit at Jesus' feet and listen to Him teach. What if Martha took as much delight in her service for the Lord as Mary did in her desiring to hear the Lord; this conversation between the Lord and Martha would not have taken place. If the Lord has given you the opportunity to do something with Him, don't get overly concerned about what others are doing; instead be satisfied that you are doing your best and that's enough.

Add your thoughts and/or prayer for the day

Luke 14:33-34
"(33) So likewise, whosoever he be of you that forsaketh not all that he hath, he cannot be my disciple. (34) Salt is good: but if the salt have lost his savour, wherewith shall it be seasoned?"

It doesn't matter what area of work a man chooses, he will never be considered good at it until he totally sells out to do his very best. In the same way a true follower of Christ knows the commitment to which he is called. Without that kind of commitment he becomes like salt that has no ability to flavor the food. The church used to be a salting agent in this country, but as we can see, something has happened; the salt has lost its savor. There is little or no commitment on the part of those who call themselves Christians. Get salty, stay committed, and sell out!

Add your thoughts and/or prayer for the day

October 27
Luke 16-18

Luke 17:9-10
"(9) Does he thank the servant because he did what was commanded? (10) So you also, when you have done all that you were commanded, say, 'We are unworthy servants; we have only done what was our duty.'"

Have you ever heard someone or maybe you have even said, "I've done all this for the Lord, where is my blessing for doing right?" Isn't it strange that in some way we feel we deserve some kind of special attention because we do what we are supposed to do? The truth is that when we do all that God has commanded through His word, all we have done is only what is the least that we can do. We have done our duty. Do right! Serve God with a pure heart in obedience and love. Be appreciative to all that the Lord has done for you. Your blessing is that you get to serve this awesome God of grace.

Add your thoughts and/or prayer for the day

October 28
Luke 19-21

Luke 19:41-42
"(41) *And when he drew near and saw the city, he wept over it, (42) saying, "Would that you, even you, had known on this day the things that make for peace! But now they are hidden from your eyes."*

Jerusalem had just received the Lord in what we call His triumphant entry, but now he weeps over the city. Why? Because they had wanted Him to be the king they wanted and not be the king He intended to be. Many want Jesus as their provider, care-giver, feel-good go-to-guy, but when it comes to being their master, Lord, and ruler of their lives, they take a pass. What is your expectation of Jesus as your Lord? Better than that, what is the Lord's expectation of you as one of His disciples and followers?

Add your thoughts and/or prayer for the day

October 29
Luke 22-24

Luke 22:61-62
"(61) And the Lord turned, and looked upon Peter. And Peter remembered the word of the Lord, how he had said unto him, Before the cock crow, thou shalt deny me thrice. (62) And Peter went out, and wept bitterly."

Peter, when caught in his sin of denial, was broken hearted that he had allowed himself to sin. With the Lord looking at him, he was overcome with guilt to the point of remorse and tears. In past generations the churches had what were called 'mourner's benches' that were placed at the front of the church where people would come, kneel and pray as they felt the guilt of their sins. Seems as though these days we can talk of sin, preach on sin, but there is no real remorse or conviction of sin. Oh how we need those old mourner's benches again with the people of God sensing a real brokenness for their sins.

Add your thoughts and/or prayer for the day

John 3:6-7
"(6) That which is born of the flesh is flesh; and that which is born of the Spirit is spirit. (7) Marvel not that I said unto thee, Ye must be born again."

Jesus explains salvation as being 'born again'. We are born of flesh that is being born the first time. Now the question is, "Have we been born of the Spirit?" That is the second birth. According to God's word we will be born of the Spirit when we put our full faith in the truth of Jesus' ability to provide for our salvation through His death, burial and resurrection. We are born in sin and need a savior. Jesus died sinless to provide us with His righteousness. He rose from the grave to demonstrate His power over death and sin. Now He offers us salvation through His grace that we receive by faith. So, have you been born again?

Add your thoughts and/or prayer for the day

October 31
John 4-6

John 6:39-40
"(39) And this is the will of him who sent me, that I should lose nothing of all that he has given me, but raise it up on the last day. (40) For this is the will of my Father, that everyone who looks on the Son and believes in him should have eternal life, and I will raise him up on the last day."

Salvation is found in none other than Jesus Christ. This salvation that is offered is eternal and it can not to be lost because first of all it is God's will that you have it. Secondly, how can anyone doubt the ability of God to save a person and then keep that person? Jesus says 'I will raise him up on the last day', that sounds like a promise and the Lord keeps His word! If you have been saved stop doubting and start living in the truth of your eternal security.

Add your thoughts and/or prayer for the day

November 1
John 7-9

John 8:7
"So when they continued asking him, he lifted up himself, and said unto them, He that is without sin among you, let him first cast a stone at her."

The story of the woman caught in adultery sure gives us a lesson on stone throwing. There is no lack of those of us who love to find fault in others, but fail to take a good look at our own failures. It makes us feel superior when we can point our fingers at others because it takes the attention off of ourselves. But the truth is that we all have sinned and fallen short of God's perfection. Instead of accusing others we should acknowledge our own sinfulness, fall own our knees confessing and then receive the forgiveness of sin that only our Savior can give. Something to think about the next time we feel like throwing stones.

Add your thoughts and/or prayer for the day

John 12:27-28
"(27) Now is my soul troubled; and what shall I say? Father, save me from this hour: but for this cause came I unto this hour. (28) Father, glorify thy name. Then came there a voice from heaven, saying, I have both glorified it, and will glorify it again."

Jesus was facing the coming temptation of his betrayal, trial and crucifixion and in His humanity He would have desired not to go through it, but in His spirit He knew it was God's plan. You may be faced with an unavoidable obstacle that you wish you did not have to face, but be sure to know that in it is the possibility for the Father to be glorified and you to be the victor. Of course that is contingent on your willingness to trust Him by faith in the moment of your doubt. God will bring glory; you just stay the course in faith.

Add your thoughts and/or prayer for the day

November 3
John 13-15

John 15:5
*"I am the vine, ye are the branches: He that abideth in me,
and I in him, the same bringeth forth much fruit: for without
me ye can do nothing."*

Here is the message of how to live the Christian life successfully, simply put, stay connected to the Lord! Our ability to do anything is dependent upon our relationship with Christ. Without Him we cannot produce anything of any value. It is through His life giving power that we can overcome sin, produce spiritual fruit, and exist as true followers of Jesus. Never become disconnected by trusting in your own ability, which only leads to failure, sin, and misery. Stay connected to the source of your joy, strength and contentment!

Add your thoughts and/or prayer for the day

November 4
John 16-18

John 17:15-17
"(15) I pray not that thou shouldest take them out of the world, but that thou shouldest keep them from the evil. (16) They are not of the world, even as I am not of the world. (17) Sanctify them through thy truth: thy word is truth."

Sometimes as a Christian we might wish we could just leave this world, but the Lord prayed that we would stay, that we might be in the world but not of the world. What will hold us in separation from the evil of the world is the word of God. As we consume the word of God it will have the affect of turning our hearts toward Him and His holiness. That in turn will separate us from the world as it seeks its own. Stay in the word! It is your sanctification.

Add your thoughts and/or prayer for the day

November 5
John 19-21

John 19:30
"When Jesus therefore had received the vinegar, he said, It is finished: and he bowed his head, and gave up the ghost."

The final words of Jesus translated 'It is finished' comes from a Greek word that actually was a term used to describe the finished transaction or as one might say, 'paid in full'. There on the cross a great transaction took place as Jesus made the final and only payment that could be made for our sins as He gave His life for ours. After becoming sin for us, He cries out to the Father that the deal is completed. Now, because of that transaction, we can come to Christ and exchange our filthy rags of self righteousness for the robe of God's righteousness that was bought and paid for by Jesus.

Add your thoughts and/or prayer for the day

November 6
Acts 1-3

Acts 2:23-24
"(23) Him, being delivered by the determinate counsel and foreknowledge of God, ye have taken, and by wicked hands have crucified and slain: (24) Whom God hath raised up, having loosed the pains of death: because it was not possible that he should be holden of it."

There has been discussion about who was responsible for killing Jesus, but the Bible is clear that His death was determined by God Himself although carried out by those who crucified Him. Don't let that surprise you, because it was God's plan from before He ever created anything. But also in that plan was the part that says death could not hold Him. Just as God had determined Christ's death, He also provided for His resurrection! What an awesome and mighty God we serve.

Add your thoughts and/or prayer for the day

Acts 5:28-29
"(28) Saying, Did not we straitly command you that ye should not teach in this name? and, behold, ye have filled Jerusalem with your doctrine, and intend to bring this man's blood upon us. (29) Then Peter and the other apostles answered and said, We ought to obey God rather than men."

The Jewish leadership was forbidding the disciples to teach of Jesus. In our day and time we have seen a rise in antagonism against Christianity to the point that our government has on many occasion stood against us trying to stop our prayers, our teaching on morality, and the truth of the Bible. In this we must be resolved to respond as did Peter, we will choose to obey God rather than man. But be sure when we stand, we will stand in opposition and persecution as we approach these last days, but let us stand!

Add your thoughts and/or prayer for the day

November 8
Acts 7-9

Acts 9:21-22
"(21) And all who heard him were amazed and said, "Is not this the man who made havoc in Jerusalem of those who called upon this name? And has he not come here for this purpose, to bring them bound before the chief priests?" (22) But Saul increased all the more in strength, and confounded the Jews who lived in Damascus by proving that Jesus was the Christ."

This is the testimony of Paul's conversion and what a conversion it was! This man's life was totally and radically changed when he met the Lord. By his own testimony, at that point, he was made into a 'new creature'. God is still in the life changing business! If a person wants to be changed, delivered from being driven by self and sin, God is ready to make that change in them. The invitation is open to all who will believe.

Add your thoughts and/or prayer for the day

November 9
Acts 10-12

Acts 10:42-43
"(42) And he commanded us to preach unto the people, and to testify that it is he which was ordained of God to be the Judge of quick and dead. (43) To him give all the prophets witness, that through his name whosoever believeth in him shall receive remission of sins."

Peter, preaching to a gentile crowd, explains the work of God as Jesus had taught the apostles. First there is the method we are to share the word of God; that is to preach, testify, and be a witness. Then he told of the message; Jesus will judge the living and the dead. His judgment is inescapable but that if anyone will believe in Him, they shall be forgiven of all their sin. The method and the message have never changed and this work of God still offers to everyone the forgiveness of sin and eternal life.

Add your thoughts and/or prayer for the day

November 10
Acts 13-15

Acts 13:38-39
"(38) Let it be known to you therefore, brothers, that through this man (Jesus) forgiveness of sins is proclaimed to you, (39) and by him everyone who believes is freed from everything from which you could not be freed by the law of Moses."

These two verses describe the message of Paul as he preached throughout his missionary journeys. This message is still the same for today, God has not changed it and it is so relevant for those who are seeking truth in their lives. Jesus Christ came to offer forgiveness for our sins through His death on the cross. Those who will put their faith in Him will find freedom from sin and from the drudgery of trying to prove one's self good enough for Heaven. God will give you a new heart that will want to seek Him not by the law but by His love.

Add your thoughts and/or prayer for the day

November 11
Acts 16-18

Acts 16:29-31
"(29) Then he called for a light, and sprang in, and came trembling, and fell down before Paul and Silas, (30) And brought them out, and said, Sirs, what must I do to be saved? (31) And they said, Believe on the Lord Jesus Christ, and thou shalt be saved, and thy house."

The Philippian jailor asks the right question to anyone who realizes they are lost in their sin. "What must I do to be saved?" The only action that a person must 'do' to be saved according to Paul was that of believing. There is no action that we can ever do in our own strength or ability that can bring us salvation. It is only in the action of faith that we believe that Jesus did enough in dying for us and then He being raised from the dead gives us assurance of that salvation. What must you do? Believe!

<u>Add your thoughts and/or prayer for the day</u>

November 12
Acts 19-21

Acts 20:24
"But none of these things move me, neither count I my life dear unto myself, so that I might finish my course with joy, and the ministry, which I have received of the Lord Jesus, to testify the gospel of the grace of God."

Paul was so totally committed to the calling of God upon his life that nothing was going to deter him from finishing the task that God had put before him. This is the kind of commitment that comes when a person falls in love with the Lord. Anyone that will give their heart and life to the Lord, can and will be used to reach others and be a witness to the grace of Christ. That is our calling, how committed are you to it?

Add your thoughts and/or prayer for the day

November 13
Acts 22-24

Acts 24:25
"And as he reasoned of righteousness, temperance, and judgment to come, Felix trembled, and answered, Go thy way for this time; when I have a convenient season, I will call for thee."

Felix was a Roman official who had imprisoned Paul and was now giving audience to him. As he listens, it is evident that Paul's message concerning faith in Christ was convicting him. Instead of yielding to the Spirit of God, he puts Him off by dismissing Paul and his message to a later time. There are those who will forfeit the peace of God by putting it off to a later time, but like Felix will never find the time to come again to that place of conviction. When the Lord speaks to us we should be quick to obey and yield to His calling.

Add your thoughts and/or prayer for the day

November 14
Acts 25-28

Acts 28:27
"For the heart of this people is waxed gross, and their ears are dull of hearing, and their eyes have they closed; lest they should see with their eyes, and hear with their ears, and understand with their heart, and should be converted, and I should heal them."

It is common today for people to refuse to listen or to make excuses for not listening to the word of God. With preconceived ideas that have been fostered by humanistic philosophy and outright lies against the truth of God's word, they not only refuse but even attack those who carry the message of God's grace and truth. What Paul saw from the Jews in Rome we are now seeing in our own society. If you have closed your heart and mind to the truth of God's word, wake up and be turned back to the truth. Jesus is the Truth!

Add your thoughts and/or prayer for the day

November 15
Romans 1-3

Romans 3:23-25
"(23) For all have sinned and fall short of the glory of God, (24) and are justified by his grace as a gift, through the redemption that is in Christ Jesus, (25) whom God put forward as a propitiation by his blood, to be received by faith. This was to show God's righteousness, because in his divine forbearance he had passed over former sins."

Very simply put, we are sinners and cannot save ourselves. Salvation comes as a gift of God's grace which was purchased by the blood sacrifice of Jesus and we receive it by faith, the forgiveness of sins. It is not through acts of our own works that save us, but through the finished work of Jesus for us. God loves you! Jesus died for you! He will save you! Believe it!

Add your thoughts and/or prayer for the day

Romans 4:20-22
"(20) He staggered not at the promise of God through unbelief; but was strong in faith, giving glory to God; (21) And being fully persuaded that, what he had promised, he was able also to perform. (22) And therefore it was imputed to him for righteousness."

This is speaking of Abraham, a man of real faith. People fail in their faith because they do not fully trust God. In some way they believe God will not do what He says He will do. Amazingly, throughout history, God has never failed to keep His promises. If God commands it, then we can believe it, for He will complete it in us, through us or for us. Find your faith in the one that does not lie, but always keeps His word.

Add your thoughts and/or prayer for the day

Romans 8:38-39
"(38) For I am persuaded, that neither death, nor life, nor angels, nor principalities, nor powers, nor things present, nor things to come, (39) Nor height, nor depth, nor any other creature, shall be able to separate us from the love of God, which is in Christ Jesus our Lord."

Oh how awesome is this Savior and God that we have that His love ascends and descends to every level of our existence. His love is so powerful that it is not hampered or made conditional on any circumstance of life we might experience. His love-hold on us cannot be broken at all! You are loved, dear child of God; loved with an unconditional, all encompassing, unrelenting passionate love! No one has or will ever love you like Jesus! Now the question is, 'How's your love for Him?'

Add your thoughts and/or prayer for the day

November 18
Romans 10-12

Romans 11:33-34
"(33) O the depth of the riches both of the wisdom and knowledge of God! how unsearchable are his judgments, and his ways past finding out! (34) For who hath known the mind of the Lord? or who hath been his counsellor?"

Isn't it just amazing that we who were created want to give counsel and instruction to the one who created us? We should rejoice over the fact that God knows more than we do, but so often we hear those who won't believe in God because they can't understand what He is doing. He is God! His thoughts go so far beyond our thoughts and His ways beyond our understanding. The great thing is that He uses His supernatural wisdom and power for the good of His creation; for our good! We don't have to know or understand what the Lord is doing. We just need to accept by faith that whatever He has allowed in our life is there to help us learn more of Him which in turn deepens our relationship with Him!

Add your thoughts and/or prayer for the day

November 19
Romans 13-16

Romans 15:5-6
"(5) Now the God of patience and consolation grant you to be likeminded one toward another according to Christ Jesus: (6) That ye may with one mind and one mouth glorify God, even the Father of our Lord Jesus Christ."

It is in our unity as believers that God can be glorified. Oh how the enemy has so divided us. Instead of divided by the doctrine or truth of God's word we find that as believers we divide over issues of uniqueness or preference. God has called us to unity. One can only imagine the glory God could receive and the good that could be done if only the Church of Jesus Christ were to come together, work together, love each other and stand for their Savior, Jesus Christ.

Add your thoughts and/or prayer for the day

November 20
1 Corinthians 1-3

1 Corinthians 1:17-18
"(17) For Christ sent me not to baptize, but to preach the gospel: not with wisdom of words, lest the cross of Christ should be made of none effect. (18) For the preaching of the cross is to them that perish foolishness; but unto us which are saved it is the power of God."

Sometimes the most important message of Christ is lost in the religious acts of man's religion. Paul here declares what is the most important and that is the message of the cross. Jesus Christ came and lived a sinless life only to be crucified, laid in a tomb for three days and then to be resurrected to life. This is the gospel and the message is that He did that for us who are sinners. Dying He paid the debt for our sin and rising from death He demonstrates His power over sin's death grip. He and He alone has the power to save us, not our church affiliation or our religious acts, but Jesus Christ Himself. It is received by faith in Him.

Add your thoughts and/or prayer for the day

November 21
1 Corinthians 4-6

1 Corinthians 6:12
"All things are lawful unto me, but all things are not expedient: all things are lawful for me, but I will not be brought under the power of any."

In the church today, this idea of libertinism is a growing problem. These are people who are declaring their spirituality superior to others based on the fact of how much liberty they have and take in the name of grace. However, according to Paul, the spiritual person is the one that knows how to restrain from taking liberty with questionable things in order to be a true witness for Christ. He especially warns against taking liberty with anything that in any way would have power over you, anything that would hinder you from thinking clearly or could be addictive. Have you been taking liberty with things that fall into this category? Be careful.

Add your thoughts and/or prayer for the day

November 22
1 Corinthians 7-9

1 Corinthians 7:22-24
"(22) For he that is called in the Lord, being a servant, is the Lord's freeman: likewise also he that is called, being free, is Christ's servant. (23) Ye are bought with a price; be not ye the servants of men. (24) Brethren, let every man, wherein he is called, therein abide with God."

The Lord has purchased us from the slavery and bondage that sin had put us under to make us free and we are free indeed! At the same time, being free, we should want to make ourselves His servants in response to His awesome grace shown to us. When it comes right down to it, we should serve Him not men. As the psalmist says in Psalms 100, "Serve the LORD with gladness: come before his presence with singing. Know ye that the LORD he is God: it is he that hath made us, and not we ourselves; we are his people, and the sheep of his pasture."

Add your thoughts and/or prayer for the day

November 23
1 Corinthians 10-12

1 Corinthians 10:13
"There hath no temptation taken you but such as is common to man: but God is faithful, who will not suffer you to be tempted above that ye are able; but will with the temptation also make a way to escape, that ye may be able to bear it."

What a promise from God for those of us who struggle with sin and the temptation of sin. First it is common to all. We are all tempted and there is no sin in temptation. It is in the yielding to the temptation that sin takes its course. So when temptation comes, it is time to look for the escape that God provides! God is faithful to provide the escape, the question is, "are we faithful to take it?"

Add your thoughts and/or prayer for the day

November 24
1 Corinthians 13-16

1 Corinthians 15:51-52
"(51) Behold, I shew you a mystery; We shall not all sleep, but we shall all be changed, (52) In a moment, in the twinkling of an eye, at the last trump: for the trumpet shall sound, and the dead shall be raised incorruptible, and we shall be changed."

This is the promise of the Lord that He will return for His church, it is referred to as the rapture. Rather by the rapture or by natural death, we shall be changed. These old bodies that we struggle to keep under submission and out of sickness or disease, they will finally be changed into bodies that will never experience aging or sickness. Best of all, they will not have an old sin nature. Temptation will have no power any longer! Sin will forever be gone from our lives. How awesome will that be?

Add your thoughts and/or prayer for the day

November 25
2 Corinthians 1-3

2 Corinthians 2:10-11
"(10) To whom ye forgive any thing, I forgive also: for if I forgave any thing, to whom I forgave it, for your sakes forgave I it in the person of Christ; Lest Satan should get an advantage of us: for we are not ignorant of his devices."

There is a truth tucked into this passage that we need in order to live in victory, it is the lesson of forgiveness. If we carry around an attitude of unforgiveness toward anyone, it only gives Satan access to our heart and it weakens us to the point of being overcome by the enemy. When we forgive, we find victory; we also find peace within ourselves. Forgiveness may benefit the one to whom it is offered, but even more, it benefits the one who offers it. When someone offends you, be quick to forgive, there is the victory!

Add your thoughts and/or prayer for the day

November 26
2 Corinthians 4-6

2 Corinthians 5:14-15
"(14) For the love of Christ constraineth us; because we thus judge, that if one died for all, then were all dead: (15) And that he died for all, that they which live should not henceforth live unto themselves, but unto him which died for them, and rose again."

The love the Lord has for us is overwhelming. It is the life changer for every believer. Understanding, accepting and walking in His love will totally transform a person. When before, we would walk in our own desires, selfishly choosing only what would benefit ourselves, now it is a whole new life! A life dedicated to living for the one who died for us. The love of Christ truly changes everything!

Add your thoughts and/or prayer for the day

Corinthians 10:17-18
"(17) But he that glorieth, let him glory in the Lord. (18) For not he that commendeth himself is approved, but whom the Lord commendeth."

Dying to self requires that we neglect promoting ourselves. Sometimes the hardest thing to do is to know how much you have done and not get any recognition for it. Or worse yet is that someone else gets the recognition for what you have done. Finding your satisfaction in the Lord should be the answer to self promotion. Letting God get the glory whether through you or someone else, what matters is that the Lord be glorified. So if you have felt insignificant and unappreciated, stop and give God the praise that He deserves for what He has done through you; He knows and that is all that matters.

Add your thoughts and/or prayer for the day

2 Corinthians 12:7-9
"(7) And lest I should be exalted above measure through the abundance of the revelations, there was given to me a thorn in the flesh, the messenger of Satan to buffet me, lest I should be exalted above measure. (8) For this thing I besought the Lord thrice, that it might depart from me. (9) And he said unto me, My grace is sufficient for thee: for my strength is made perfect in weakness. Most gladly therefore will I rather glory in my infirmities, that the power of Christ may rest upon me."

Sometimes the very things we would wish were not in our lives are the very things God wants to use to show us His grace. Which would you rather have a life without problems or a life upon which the power of Christ rests? According to Paul, we should glory in our weaknesses, the places we are insufficient, because in them we will experience the strength and power of God's grace!

Add your thoughts and/or prayer for the day

November 29
Galatians 1-3

Galatians 2:16
*"Knowing that a man is not justified by the works of the law,
but by the faith of Jesus Christ, even we have believed in
Jesus Christ, that we might be justified by the faith of Christ,
and not by the works of the law: for by the works of the law
shall no flesh be justified."*

How frustrating it is to try and live up to the law of God, trying in some way to be good enough to receive eternal life. [It is clear in scripture that the law was given to reveal our need for a savior. Eternal life is received by faith in the finished work of Jesus as He was crucified for our sins, buried and then rose from death as victor over sin. His death offers us that which we cannot earn, eternal life.] Aren't you glad that our salvation doesn't depend upon what we can do, but on what Christ did for us?

Add your thoughts and/or prayer for the day

Galatians 4:4-7
*"(4) But when the fulness of the time was come, God sent
forth his Son, made of a woman, made under the law, to
redeem them that were under the law, that we might receive
the adoption of sons. Wherefore thou art no more a servant,
but a son; and if a son, then an heir of God through Christ."*

Wow! When we could not save ourselves from our sin, God
sent us His Son, Jesus, to redeem us from our sin. Then He
offers to adopt us into His family through our reception of
Jesus as our Lord. Then we are no longer slaves to our sin,
but become children of God! We become heirs of eternal
life through our faith in Jesus Christ; Sons and daughters
of God! Isn't that just the most awesome thing you could
ever experience?

Add your thoughts and/or prayer for the day

December 1
Ephesians 1-3

Ephesians 3:17-19
"(17) That Christ may dwell in your hearts by faith; that ye, being rooted and grounded in love, (18) May be able to comprehend with all saints what is the breadth, and length, and depth, and height; (19) And to know the love of Christ, which passeth knowledge, that ye might be filled with all the fulness of God."

The love of Christ, what a gift of grace! It is immeasurable, inconceivable, unconditional, and irrational but it is ours in Him! When everything in our lives may seem to be falling apart or have no purpose, we can anchor to the love Christ has for us. Without explanation, we find that we are overwhelmed, filled to overflowing with our Lord's love for us. If you are having a pity party today, stop and realize how much you are loved by your Lord.

Add your thoughts and/or prayer for the day

December 2
Ephesians 4-6

Ephesians 4:31-32
"(31) Let all bitterness, and wrath, and anger, and clamour, and evil speaking, be put away from you, with all malice: (32) And be ye kind one to another, tenderhearted, forgiving one another, even as God for Christ's sake hath forgiven you."

What comes out of our mouths will reveal what is in our hearts, but even more exposing are the attitudes that keep us from genuine love for others. If we have been truly born again in Christ, His Spirit will manifest Himself through us by the way we treat others. It doesn't matter what your personality is, there should be tenderheartedness, a kindness and a forgiving spirit that is seen and overwhelms us as we deal with others. What would others say about your attitude, your spirit, is it truly Christ-like? If not, something is wrong.

Add your thoughts and/or prayer for the day

December 3
Philippians 1-4

Philippians 2:3-4 ESV
"(3) Do nothing from selfish ambition or conceit, but in humility count others more significant than yourselves. (4) Let each of you look not only to his own interests, but also to the interests of others."

It seems we live in a world of people who only look out for themselves, so busy making sure they get what they think they deserve. For the follower of Jesus Christ, we are called to a much higher calling than to just be concerned with ourselves. We are to be servants and ministers to others. Today, look for an opportunity to go out of your way to help someone else with absolutely no chance of anything in it for you. This is true "Christ likeness"! It should be our nature, being born of the Spirit, to want to give of ourselves to serve others.

Add your thoughts and/or prayer for the day

December 4
Colossians 1-4

Colossians 2:8-10
"(8) Beware lest any man spoil you through philosophy and vain deceit, after the tradition of men, after the rudiments of the world, and not after Christ. (9) For in him dwelleth all the fulness of the Godhead bodily. (10) And ye are complete in him, which is the head of all principality and power:"

As Christians we need to be aware of the pop psychology that is infiltrating the church. Messages being preached that sound good because they feed the flesh with humanistic reason, but have no root in the word of God. Our wholeness is not found in just being a better person, but in establishing Jesus as our completer, our everything. As Paul says, we are complete in Him!

Add your thoughts and/or prayer for the day

December 5
1 Thessalonians 1-3

1 Thessalonians 2:4
"But as we were allowed of God to be put in trust with the gospel, even so we speak; not as pleasing men, but God, which trieth our hearts."

Paul speaks here of the gospel as a treasure that has been entrusted to us. Is that the way we think about this glorious message of salvation; the death, burial and resurrection of Christ? To Paul this message was so important that nothing could keep him from sharing it with others. Sometimes it was received with joy and other times it was rejected with malice, but no matter the reception Paul continued to give it out because his desire was to please God. What hinders us from speaking to others this great message of promise?

Add your thoughts and/or prayer for the day

December 6
1 Thessalonians 4-5

1 Thessalonians 4:11-12
"(11) And that ye study to be quiet, and to do your own business, and to work with your own hands, as we commanded you; (12) That ye may walk honestly toward them that are without, and that ye may have lack of nothing."

Three truths to a successful life start with living quietly, meaning to be at peace with yourself, God and others. Secondly is to do your own business which is to take care of the things that concern your life not having to depend on someone else to do it for you. Thirdly, don't be afraid of work. If you do these things, the result will be a great witness to others and your needs will be supplied. Simple, right? Wonder why some folks just never get it?

Add your thoughts and/or prayer for the day

December 7
2 Thessalonians 1-3

2 Thessalonians 3:11-13
"(11) For we hear that there are some which walk among you disorderly, working not at all, but are busybodies. (12) Now them that are such we command and exhort by our Lord Jesus Christ, that with quietness they work, and eat their own bread. (13) But ye, brethren, be not weary in well doing."

Lots of people are minding everyone's business but their own and in so doing fail to accomplish what they are supposed to be doing. These 'busybodies' can rob us of our ability to do our job by their constant interruptions, but we should be driven by a higher calling that refuses to let them keep us from the joy of doing what is right. Hang in there and do not give up, victory is on its way!

Add your thoughts and/or prayer for the day

December 8
1 Timothy 1-3

1 Timothy 2:3-6
"(3) For this is good and acceptable in the sight of God our Saviour; (4) Who will have all men to be saved, and to come unto the knowledge of the truth. (5) For there is one God, and one mediator between God and men, the man Christ Jesus; (6) Who gave himself a ransom for all, to be testified in due time."

God's offer of salvation is limitless! Through the sacrifice of Jesus, God is able to save anyone and everyone that will come to Him in faith believing that Christ's death, burial and resurrection is the full payment for their sin. Please note that it is only through Jesus Christ that this ransom is made, not the church you belong to nor the works you perform. Jesus alone is our mediator, our payment, and our Savior.

Add your thoughts and/or prayer for the day

1 Timothy 6:6-8
"(6) But godliness with contentment is great gain. (7) For we brought nothing into this world, and it is certain we can carry nothing out. (8) And having food and raiment let us be therewith content."

Oh how we can get caught up on the treadmill of having stuff! The world around us continually throws the idea of material possessions as the way to happiness. Before you know it, we have bitten off a chunk of this ideology and find that it is a never ending pit of disappointment and stress just trying to keep up with it all. God, on the other hand, offers a way of peaceful living filled with satisfaction and contentment. It is not difficult to have; it is simply learning to be satisfied with what we have trusting the Lord will always provide whatever we need. Get off the treadmill and begin to enjoy all that the Lord has given you. It is more than enough and it is eternal!

Add your thoughts and/or prayer for the day

December 10
2 Timothy 1-4

2 Timothy 2:15
"Study to shew thyself approved unto God, a workman that needeth not to be ashamed, rightly dividing the word of truth."

When we were in a classroom and the teacher said we were to study a certain book or chapter, we understood that we had a responsibility to know the material for the next class. This usually required that we had read the material, became familiar with it and begun to understand it. Do you think that Paul meant the same thing here for Timothy? Well sure he did, and the same is true with us. For us to be able to rightly divide the word of truth, we need to have studied it, become familiar with it and got an understanding of it. Too many people are ready to spout what they believe, but it is obvious they don't know the material. Study dear child of God, study so you won't need to be ashamed.

Add your thoughts and/or prayer for the day

December 11
Titus 1-3

Titus 3:5-7
"(5) Not by works of righteousness which we have done, but according to his mercy he saved us, by the washing of regeneration, and renewing of the Holy Ghost; (6) Which he shed on us abundantly through Jesus Christ our Saviour; (7) That being justified by his grace, we should be made heirs according to the hope of eternal life."

How are we saved, regenerated, renewed, justified and made heirs of eternal life? Well, it is not by something we do but by the Lord's mercy and awesome grace that we receive all this. If you are still 'trying' to be good enough to go to Heaven, please listen carefully to this lesson from God's word. You won't make it on your works of righteousness, only through putting your faith in what the Lord has already done for you and offers freely by His grace.

Add your thoughts and/or prayer for the day

December 12
Philemon 1

Philemon 1:5-6
"(5) ... I hear of your love and of the faith that you have toward the Lord Jesus and for all the saints, (6) and I pray that the sharing of your faith may become effective for the full knowledge of every good thing that is in us for the sake of Christ."

Philemon is recognized by Paul for his love and faith toward Jesus and all the saints. These are the qualities that made his witness effective to others. Sometimes our witness to others is marred because they have seen in us qualities that do not line up with the story of the gospel. The gospel is more easily received when our lives have prepared the way by our demonstration of love and faith. Just remember your greatest witness for the Lord comes first from a life that others see as genuine in your commitment to Christ.

Add your thoughts and/or prayer for the day

December 13
Hebrews 1-3

Hebrews 2:14-15
"(14) Forasmuch then as the children are partakers of flesh and blood, he also himself likewise took part of the same; that through death he might destroy him that had the power of death, that is, the devil; (15) And deliver them who through fear of death were all their lifetime subject to bondage."

Jesus became a man to be a part of us so that through His death, burial and resurrection He could free us from the inescapable chains of death. Jesus has done what is necessary to give us deliverance from the devil and the power of death. Have you been delivered and set free or are you still under sin's power and Satan's control? There is freedom for the person that comes to Jesus by faith and receives God's gift of grace. This gift has been bought and paid for by the Lord's sacrifice on Calvary.

Add your thoughts and/or prayer for the day

Hebrews 4:12
"For the word of God is quick, and powerful, and sharper than any twoedged sword, piercing even to the dividing asunder of soul and spirit, and of the joints and marrow, and is a discerner of the thoughts and intents of the heart."

The one thing that is the greatest asset in the Christian's arsenal to be able to stand against the enemy is the Word of God! Your Bible has power wrapped in every page and in every word. Read it, study it, learn it, memorize it, for with it God can and will do great things in and through you. Without it, you will find yourself floundering through life never certain of anything that God is doing. Don't be satisfied with the milk of the word; seek to be a self feeder, feasting on the meat of the word.

Add your thoughts and/or prayer for the day

December 15
Hebrews 7-10

Hebrews 10:24-25
"(24) And let us consider one another to provoke unto love and to good works: (25) Not forsaking the assembling of ourselves together, as the manner of some is; but exhorting one another: and so much the more, as ye see the day approaching."

There was a time when life was simple, things moved slower and there were times to meditate on God's word and allow it to sink into our deepest thoughts, but now life moves at light speed and our minds are drawn away so easily by the ever increasing and easily accessible worldly attractions. That is why we need each other all the more in these last days to encourage us in our walk with the Lord. Recognize those things that draw you away from fellowship with the church and do not miss the opportunity to be with other believers. We need each other now more than ever before!

Add your thoughts and/or prayer for the day

December 16
Hebrews 11-13

Hebrews 12:1-2
"(1) Wherefore seeing we also are compassed about with so great a cloud of witnesses, let us lay aside every weight, and the sin which doth so easily beset us, and let us run with patience the race that is set before us, (2) Looking unto Jesus the author and finisher of our faith; who for the joy that was set before him endured the cross, despising the shame, and is set down at the right hand of the throne of God."

We have the witness of all those who successfully lived a life of faith in Christ. We also have the example of our commander and chief, Jesus himself who demonstrated for us the life totally surrendered to God. The only thing that can defeat us is the sin of unbelief and taking our eyes off of the Lord. Stay in the battle, do not give up, the Lord is in sight!

Add your thoughts and/or prayer for the day

December 17
James 1-3

James 3:15-17
"(15) This wisdom descendeth not from above, but is earthly, sensual, devilish. (16) For where envying and strife is, there is confusion and every evil work. (17) But the wisdom that is from above is first pure, then peaceable, gentle, and easy to be intreated, full of mercy and good fruits, without partiality, and without hypocrisy."

Two kinds of wisdom listed here. One produces confusion, strife and division, the other mercy, genuine care for others and a life consumed with honesty. Which one describes you? Determining this, you will know from whose household you are receiving instruction. Our wisdom should come from above; from the household of faith. Being a person of godly wisdom will result in finding real peace and joy. Seek wisdom, but seek the right kind of wisdom; the wisdom that comes from God.

<u>**Add your thoughts and/or prayer for the day**</u>

December 18
James 4-5

James 4:14-15
"(14) Whereas ye know not what shall be on the morrow. For what is your life? It is even a vapour, that appeareth for a little time, and then vanisheth away. (15) For that ye ought to say, If the Lord will, we shall live, and do this, or that."

As young people we think we have all the time in the world and as we age, we come to the realization that our time is so short. For many, the time runs out before we ever figure out just what it is that we were supposed to get done. Don't waste a minute of your time for it is not yours to waste it is the Lord's. He is the one that gives us life and each life whether short or long is given to bring honor to Him. If you're living your life for just yourself, you are selling out for too little a purpose and way too little a benefit to yourself and to others. Seek the Lord early in your lives and then walk with Him the rest of your lives. Now that is a life fulfilled!

Add your thoughts and/or prayer for the day

December 19
1 Peter 1-3

1 Peter 3:10-12
"(10) For he that will love life, and see good days, let him refrain his tongue from evil, and his lips that they speak no guile: (11) Let him eschew evil, and do good; let him seek peace, and ensue it. (12) For the eyes of the Lord are over the righteous, and his ears are open unto their prayers: but the face of the Lord is against them that do evil."

It should not surprise us that the Lord in all His holiness does not tolerate sin. Yet it is surprising that those who would hate God's order would be those that cry the loudest that they feel in some way God is unjust when we suffer for our unrighteousness. God made man to live in obedience to Him and when we do, we are blessed. When we choose to live in opposition to His commands, we will suffer. It really is just that simple!

Add your thoughts and/or prayer for the day

December 20
1 Peter 4-5

1 Peter 5:10
"But the God of all grace, who hath called us unto his eternal glory by Christ Jesus, after that ye have suffered a while, make you perfect, stablish, strengthen, settle you."

When suffering comes our way it is there for one of two reasons. It can be a result of sin and God lovingly chastening us back into fellowship with Him or it can be a time of faith building as God schools us in trusting Him. In either case we find that suffering is one of God's greatest tools to building our faith. So when those times of suffering come, instead of complaining just stay focused on all that you have in Christ and rejoice for all that He is doing in your life through this classroom experience and GROW!

Add your thoughts and/or prayer for the day

December 21
2 Peter 1-3

2 Peter 3:13-14
"(13) Nevertheless we, according to his promise, look for new heavens and a new earth, wherein dwelleth righteousness. (14) Wherefore, beloved, seeing that ye look for such things, be diligent that ye may be found of him in peace, without spot, and blameless."

In the movie "Hoosiers" the coach tells his players to not "get caught watching the paint dry". Here Peter warns us that as we are waiting on what we know is coming, a new heaven and new earth, that we should not get so caught up in the waiting that we forget that we have a purpose to fulfill. God has saved us to bring Him glory, not just sit around and wait for His coming. Let your life count by being found in a vibrant, life altering, joy producing relationship with the Lord.

Add your thoughts and/or prayer for the day

December 22
1 John 1-3

1 John 2:4-6
"(4) He that saith, I know him, and keepeth not his commandments, is a liar, and the truth is not in him. (5) But whoso keepeth his word, in him verily is the love of God perfected: hereby know we that we are in him. (6) He that saith he abideth in him ought himself also so to walk, even as he walked."

According to the word of God there is evidence that is seen in those who truly know the Savior. Our desire should be to live in obedience to the Lord's commands and allowing His love to penetrate every area of our lives with a true heart. So there is the truth of the matter; our love for the Lord and our relationship to Him should be so invested that where He walks that is where we will be.

Add your thoughts and/or prayer for the day

December 23
1 John 4 – 2 John 1

1 John 5:11-13
"(11) And this is the record, that God hath given to us eternal life, and this life is in his Son. (12) He that hath the Son hath life; and he that hath not the Son of God hath not life. (13) These things have I written unto you that believe on the name of the Son of God; that ye may know that ye have eternal life, and that ye may believe on the name of the Son of God."

According to the Bible, if you have the Son you have life and should know that you have eternal life. So the question is very simple, "Do you have the Son?" Receiving Jesus (John 1:12) means to put your trust in the fact that He died for your sins and through His death, burial, and resurrection He has complete forgiveness for you (Colossians 2:13-14). If you have never received this forgiveness, God stands ready to give it to you right now, just ask Him. If you walk in this forgiveness, share it with others!

Add your thoughts and/or prayer for the day

December 24
3 John 1 – Jude 1

Jude 1:11
"Woe unto them! for they have gone in the way of Cain, and ran greedily after the error of Balaam for reward, and perished in the gainsaying of Core."

Jude warns of the apostate preachers of the last days and he uses three men to describe their character. Cain, who brought his own work before the Lord and expected it to be received with honor; Balaam, a prophet who was driven by the lust for money; Core (Korah), driven by a lust for power, who led a rebellion against Moses, the man of God. One doesn't have to look far to find men who stand in pulpits promoting themselves, preaching whatever needs to be said in order to build their little kingdoms and rebelling against any accountability from real men of God. Be careful dear child of God to the apostates of the last days.

Add your thoughts and/or prayer for the day

Revelation 1-3

Revelation 3:19-20
"(19) As many as I love, I rebuke and chasten: be zealous therefore, and repent. (20) Behold, I stand at the door, and knock: if any man hear my voice, and open the door, I will come in to him, and will sup with him, and he with me."

We can see how the 21st century church fits this description of the end time's church. The church has become an entertainment center where we have turned to every kind of worldly attraction to promote our church and leaving the Lord on the outside looking in. God wants the church to be a lighthouse of moral character, bent on standing firm on the truth of His word, calling people out of the world to a different walk, a holy walk with Him. He is crying out to us, the church, to let him back in. This is why in the previous verses He calls for the church to "buy of me gold tried in the fire, that thou mayest be rich; and white raiment, that thou mayest be clothed, and *that* the shame of thy nakedness do not appear; and anoint thine eyes with eyesalve, that thou mayest see."

Add your thoughts and/or prayer for the day

December 26
Revelation 4-6

Revelation 5:11-12
"(11) And I beheld, and I heard the voice of many angels round about the throne and the beasts and the elders: and the number of them was ten thousand times ten thousand, and thousands of thousands; (12) Saying with a loud voice, Worthy is the Lamb that was slain to receive power, and riches, and wisdom, and strength, and honour, and glory, and blessing."

When we read this, we should understand and be awed at the fact that John saw what we shall see and participate in as Jesus the Lamb of God presents Himself to break the seals and open the book. One day, you can be sure that if you are a true child of God, you will be numbered with those listed here that will sing this powerful testimony of our Savior as we look upon Him who saved us. How awesome will that be!

Add your thoughts and/or prayer for the day

December 27
Revelation 7-9

Revelation 9:20-21
"(20) And the rest of the men which were not killed by these plagues yet repented not of the works of their hands, that they should not worship devils, and idols of gold, and silver, and brass, and stone, and of wood: which neither can see, nor hear, nor walk: (21) Neither repented they of their murders, nor of their sorceries, nor of their fornication, nor of their thefts."

It is amazing that during the seven year tribulation period described here, that with all the horrors of death, destruction, suffering and pain that the sin of men will be so great that they still will not turn to the one true God. Their hearts will turn even further away from the one who could and would save them, simply to continue to worship false gods and live in their own sin. I'm afraid we see that today, as people continue to attack the truth and hate the one who loves them.

Add your thoughts and/or prayer for the day

December 28
Revelation 10-12

Revelation 12:10-11
"(10) *And I heard a loud voice saying in heaven, Now is come salvation, and strength, and the kingdom of our God, and the power of his Christ: for the accuser of our brethren is cast down, which accused them before our God day and night.
(11) And they overcame him by the blood of the Lamb, and by the word of their testimony; and they loved not their lives unto the death.*"

Our accuser, Satan, will one day be cast out from heaven. But notice the weapons of the angels that defeat him. The blood of Christ which has the power to cleanse us from sin, a testimony which all of us have concerning the Lord's work in our lives, and by their total surrender to Him. As God's children, we have the first two for sure, now all we need is a total, sold-out, commitment to the Lord and we too can defeat old smutty face as well.

Add your thoughts and/or prayer for the day

December 29
Revelation 13-16

Revelation 15:3-4
"(3) And they sing the song of Moses the servant of God, and the song of the Lamb, saying, Great and marvellous are thy works, Lord God Almighty; just and true are thy ways, thou King of saints. (4) Who shall not fear thee, O Lord, and glorify thy name? for thou only art holy: for all nations shall come and worship before thee; for thy judgments are made manifest."

Here John hears the angelic chorus singing of the truth of God even as they are carrying out the judgment of God. God never gives up on the offer of His grace, even while pouring out judgment, His love is offered in grace. God will punish sin and He will be righteous and faithful in His chastisement. However, God's love is unfailing through all of this and His offer of salvation is always available. He would have all come to repentance, which is His desire.

Add your thoughts and/or prayer for the day

December 30
Revelation 17-19

Revelation 17:13-14
"(13) These have one mind, and shall give their power and strength unto the beast. (14) These shall make war with the Lamb, and the Lamb shall overcome them: for he is Lord of lords, and King of kings: and they that are with him are called, and chosen, and faithful."

In the battle of Armageddon, the place where Satan will pull out all stops in a final attempt to destroy the Lord, the enemy will find that our Lord and King is greater than all! You are reading the end of the story and no matter what may happen now; Jesus will be victorious in the end. Those who are with Him are the redeemed of the Lord, and have found their salvation in Him. We win because we are led by the King of kings and the Lord of lords! Hallelujah to our King, King Jesus!

Add your thoughts and/or prayer for the day

Revelation 20:14-15
"(14) And death and hell were cast into the lake of fire. This is the second death. (15) And whosoever was not found written in the book of life was cast into the lake of fire."

Describing the final judgment called the Great White Throne judgment; all those who have continually rejected God's gift of eternal life through Christ will be brought before the Lord. It is here they will be granted their last appeal as the Lord will judge them upon the works of their life and every one of them will come up short of the righteousness required for salvation. But the Lord in His justice will then look to see if by chance their name was written in the book of life, but it won't be there because every time the Lord had given them the opportunity to receive salvation by His grace and mercy, they had turned their backs on Him. So the question is, "Is your name written in the book of life?"

Add your thoughts and/or prayer for the day

A Final Thought

Revelation 22:3-5
"(3) And there shall be no more curse: but the throne of God and of the Lamb shall be in it; and his servants shall serve him: (4) And they shall see his face; and his name shall be in their foreheads. (5) And there shall be no night there; and they need no candle, neither light of the sun; for the Lord God giveth them light: and they shall reign for ever and ever."

As we finish this reading of the scripture, we end with the promise of the eternal kingdom, the New Jerusalem and we, the bride of Christ, taking up residence there. A place with no more sin and we with no sin nature, streets of gold and gates of pearl, foundations of gemstones and the river of life .... but best of all, we will be forever in the physical presence of the one who died for us and we will worship Him with unobstructed passion. Now that is Heaven!

The Word of God is our life source! It is my desire that as you have gone through this year of devotions with me, that your heart has been stirred to continue on your own. May you find God's richest blessings as you read, study, meditate and share His word with others.

Jim Newton

Made in the USA
Charleston, SC
16 November 2015